You Must Work Harde
Poetry of Excellence

You Must Work Harder to Write Poetry of Excellence

Crafts Discourse and the Common Reader in Canadian Poetry Book Reviews

Donato Mancini

BookThug

Type+Design: www.beautifuloutlaw.com

The production of this book was made possible through the generous assistance of the Ontario Arts Council and the Canada Council for the Arts.

 ONTARIO ARTS COUNCIL
CONSEIL DES ARTS DE L'ONTARIO

 Canada Council   Conseil des Arts
for the Arts   du Canada

LIBRARY AND ARCHIVES CANADA CATALOGUING IN PUBLICATION

Mancini, Donato, [date]
You must work harder to write poetry of excellence: ideology, ideolect and aesthetic conscience in Canadian poetry reviews since 1961/ Donato Mancini.

(Department of critical thought series; no. 7)
Issued also in electronic format.
ISBN 978-1-927040-42-3

1. Canadian poetry – 20th century – Reviews. 2. Canadian poetry – 21st century – Reviews. 3. Canadian poetry – 20th century – History and criticism. 4. Canadian poetry – 21st century – History and criticism. I. Title. II. Series: Department of critical thought; no. 7

PS8141.M36 2012   C811'.5409   C2012-905412-7

PRINTED IN CANADA

Ultimately, it's all for the glory of poetry....

Table of Contents

A Retired Engineer Who Reads Houseman and Listens to Recordings of Dylan Thomas: The Tropes of Fantasy

One of the Few Genuine Remaining Hardware Stores: The Discourse of Craft

Through Canadian Poetry Reviewing

Works Cited

Here Come the Common Sense Police

Categorically Snowblind

1961. The year the postmodern breaks out in English Canadian poetry. Or, let's say, in 1961 the emergence of the postmodern into Anglophone Canadian poetry passes a significant increment. A noteworthy marker of this emergence is a review by J. R. Colombo in the December 1961 issue of *The Canadian Forum* – a prominent, left-leaning, nationally distributed magazine founded in 1920 – of a pair of zines from opposite sides of the country. He reviews *Cataract* from Montreal, and a handmade student publication from the University of British Columbia only available directly from the editors. *Tish*, Colombo notes, is "mimeographed on legal-sized stationary … fourteen pages held dexterously together with a single staple" (212). He reads the content of both zines through the political economy of Canadian publishing. When he writes, opening his review, that he "collect[s] little magazines" (211), his "little" connotes a naturalization of institutional privilege and the history of literary value. Coasting in the always ideological register of the Obvious, Colombo's review teems with potentially malign, circular assumptions. Real poets write real poetry. Real poetry is good poetry. Which poetry is good? The poetry in the good (= big budget) magazines. Quality is legible: Read it. So Colombo relates that:

After reading the first two issues of Tish, *and the most recent issue of* Cataract, *I have come to the conclusion that there is a type of poem known as the 'little magazine poem.' There is a vast graveyard on the periphery of American letters known as 'little magazine literature.' This graveyard is in-*

habited by ghosts whose work will appear and reappear in little magazines from now to kingdom come, but as writers they will never appear in broad daylight, because as 'work' their writing does not really exist. Hence there is such a thing as the 'little magazine poet,' but happily Canada has had few of these. Of course good poets occasionally publish in little magazines, but invariably their best work never appears in the barely legible mimeo mag pages: it is reserved for the quality or mass magazines. (212)

Here, Colombo uses contrasting temporal tropes to devaluate poetry produced outside of what Charles Bernstein has called "official verse culture." Versus the "built-in obsolescence" of zines, true poetry is found in consecrated publications such as "*Canadian Literature* and the *University of Toronto Quarterly* [that] look like they will continue forever" (212). The poetry in little magazines is not real poetry. Unsanctioned, it "does not really exist." Otherwise, why does Colombo characterize the periphery of official verse culture a "graveyard"? Nor do the little magazine writers "really exist." Marginal writers are the uncounted dead of literary history, collateral damage in the long forward march of official culture. Like the poor, they will be with official culture until "kingdom come." Zines' "obsession with the present" (212), rather than a more licit obsession with fantasies of posterity or reverent attitudes to official tradition, dooms them to live a continuous past tense, to live as ghosts. Although as an editor and writer, Colombo has made major contributions to inventive postmodern poetry in Canada, (and in analyzing this review, I make no claims about Colombo's other writings, nor about his person), in this specific review the language of value – the *ideolect* – has baleful connotations. Here, it seems, Colombo collects little magazines like a colonial anthropologist collects human skulls.

Quite a problematic specimen, Colombo's review is signal for that very reason. Note that, although he judges the poetry in *Cataract* as superior, he gives twice as much print space wholly to *Tish* for being "more lively." One remark in particular anticipates several key debate points of the poetry wars of the coming decades, in which *Tish* serves as an important (if upvalued) token. He writes:

The curious feature of Tish *is that it is 'beat.' It seems a bit strange to read in a Vancouver magazine a longish essay about the poetics of Philip Whalen, and to struggle over such phrases as the 'natural association of object/ action/ words.'* (212)

Curious, Colombo suggests, that a Canadian poetry magazine would draw influence from non-Canadian ("beat") sources. Strange to "struggle over" these young writers' attempts to worm their way out of dominant Canadian literary ideology, into the nervous, insecure territory of new poetics. (Note the *Tish*-ite master trope of Olsonian "proprioception" emergent in the formulation that, like many after him, Colombo trips over.) Lively, beat *Tish* soon creates a surprisingly intense furore in Canadian poetry. Colombo's review – its air of majesterial generosity notwithstanding – indeed shows acuity about the cultural moment: The "cultural revolution" of postmodern poetry is coming on, even if this revolution, as he believes, is "imported" and "a bit late" (212).

Canadian poetry from that period onwards – since this postmodern turn, or emergence – pluralizes into such a multitude of contradictory, antagonistic practices that it becomes not only a different cultural field, but Canadian poetry becomes an altogether different concept. Astonishing, therefore, how many of the assumptions that govern reviews like Colombo's persist in poetry book reviews today. Poetry practice has thoroughly transformed, while the ideolect (i.e., the tropes, metaphors, concepts, and critical frameworks) of poetry reviews current 50 years ago remains substantially unchanged. Poetry reviewing in Canada has not even minimally kept up with its putative object.

In a round-up review of all the poetry titles nominated for the Governor General's award in 2007, Steven Laird, author of three poetry collections, casts his gaze across the Canadian poetic field:

13

Let's call the [Governor General's Award] a litmus test of what our writers have perfected: if so, then these books demonstrate that the lyric is king, all the difficult knots have been mastered, and the "I" that loves to speak the poems is alive, alert, and secure in its place. I've read each of these books with varying degrees of pleasure. Yet, in the end, there's something either missing or very tired in the ideas – not the skill – that drives them. (21)

Almost 50 years on, Laird reproduces some of the most problematic assumptions found in Colombo's 1961 review of *Tish* and *Cataract*. Even his phrase "our writers" is suspect. It assumes a consensus on literary value which the GG lists unproblematically project, and assumes that the national aesthetic identity of Canadian readers is largely unitary. Laird elides that in the entire period since 1961, hundreds of Canadian poets have risen from bed each day self-tasked only to conspire against the values of official verse culture, to depose poetry's lyric "king." Laird has it as Colombo had it: Only such permanent, opulent bodies as the Canada Council have the power of literary consecration until kingdom come. His observation of something "either missing or very tired in the [lyric poets'] ideas" directly echoes observations which poets across North America had already made (bitterly) when those two first issues of *Tish* roll out of the Gestetner. In the view of many poets, the forms of literary subjecthood presumed in the self-assured lyric I "secure in its place" steadily erode through the 1960s. In this view, the continued production of lyric poems is anachronistic. The cultural conditions and relations of production, emergent after the so-called postmodern turn, disintegrate the social subject I posited in lyric poetry. After this turn, lyric poetry can only have continued pertinence (if any pertinence at all) within the ideological terms of a contested literary field. Radically non-lyrical alternative poetries have to develop, to give lyric poetry a productively defining antagonist, or there remains no reason for it to exist. And those alternatives develop abundantly: Today, a large internationally recognized body of Canadian poetry exists not premised, formally, aesthetically or morally, in the self-assured Romantic subject. But, as Colombo suggest-

14

ed in 1961 – in spite of his own later poetic and editing contributions – writers unconsecrated by official verse culture, with all their concerns, investigations, poetics, all their new values, "don't really exist." With all the breadth of Laird's gaze, which borrows the eyes of a national cultural ideology, it cannot see any of the other territories of Canadian poetry. Does this mean Laird represents a sector of Canadian poetry with its cultural calendar set to New Year's Eve 1958? Or has Canadian poetry review criticism, compasses thrown off by the magnesis of postmodernity, circled in a blizzard for 50 years? Categorically snowblind?

The University of British Columbia is not, of course, the only place in Vancouver where challenges to official Canadian verse culture are pursued in the 1960s. In the downtown core, many proprioceptive miles from the culture of the school, numerous poets of an unofficial drift, most of whom are unconnected with academia, produce and distribute their own writings. These writers include: Judith Copithorne, bill bissett, Gerry Gilbert, Maxine Gadd and Roy Kiyooka. *Tish* is only a signal and symptom of broader changes taking place across the country, for which it becomes a conveniently reductive token in the construction of Canadian literary history. Certainly, from the early 1960s on, postmodern poetry has increased its hold on the material means of self-reproduction – presses, magazines, institutional affiliations, grants, distribution networks, sales figures, transnational poetic communities. George Bowering wins his first Governor General's award for poetry in 1969 with *Gangs of Kosmos* and *Rocky Mountain Foot*; the following year the prize goes jointly to bpNichol and Michael Ondaatje. Robin Blaser wins a Griffin Prize in 2006 in the form of a Lifetime Recognition Award, then in 2008 receives the prize again for his collected poems, *The Holy Forest*. At least five of Canada's best-selling, and most internationally recognized, poets write in a postmodern vein: Lisa Robertson, Erín Moure, Christian Bök, Steve McCaffery and M. Nourbese Philip. A growing number of such poets have tenured positions in Canadian universities. Postmodernity has indelibly marked and transformed the Canadian poetic field.

Opening of (the Rifts in) the Field

In an interview by a member of the Seminary Co-op Bookstore in Chicago, Charles Bernstein gives a tart definition of his term "official verse culture":

The problem with official verse culture, what makes it official, is its unreflected assertion of centrality. Official verse culture's appropriation of an imaginary center operates through its a series of exclusions of the bulk of ... the most active and engaging work being done. This ends up giving poetry a bad name, makes it seem a dull art for genteel readers. ("Interview")

In the defining antagonisms between the central and the marginal, the postmodern and the "permamodern" (as in "permafrost") open the materially lived rifts in the field of Canadian poetry. [I generally mean antagonistic, and antagonism, in the sense meant by Ernesto Laclau: "[In] an antagonistic relation there is the peculiar possibility that the object, the entity that I am, is negated." (256)] From 1961 onwards, the topography of the field becomes increasingly uneven.

Most notably, two broad territories or camps are established, each premised on divergent interpretations of history (social and literary), and of contemporaneity. The relationship between these territories is porous, nothing like a binary relationship. To consider for a moment the analogy of the cultural field: The relationship between antagonistic positions or territories in a cultural field, although sometimes antagonistic, is porous. Winnipeg can be compared to Windsor, for example, their distinctiveness marked, but they do not become in this comparison the 1 and 0 of a sealed binary. Field relationships are non-static, evolutionary/developmental without being impermeably exclusive, progressive or teleological. Evolution does not move "forward" or "progress." It is a process of transformative adaptation to changing conditions, not a process of essential refinement (i.e., evolution doesn't build a better cane toad). The antagonisms that produce such changes are not binary, but multiply relative.

Although this study aims to tear at the roots of a national cultural ideology, it does not pretend to cover all the internal tensions, discordances, divisions, contradictions and antagonisms, all the pluralities of the Canadian poetic field within these two territories, or beyond. I cannot claim to adequately address practices of opposition to official verse culture premised and practiced on entirely other terms than these ideolectical struggles I analyze here. The most egregious omission is, arguably, the range of racialized poetic practices – including dub, hip hop, spoken word, performance poetry, indigenous writing, racialised feminist writing – that develop with special intensity in the 1980s, (predictably) subjected to either silencing, or exclusion, or adjudicative condemnation, or to political neutralisation (a.k.a., race management) by ideological praise. From *both* poetic camps.

In a review of Louise Bernice Halfe's *Blue Marrow* (1998), for example, Theresa Shea makes some typical discriminating moves, distinguishing the sociological or historical interest of Halfe's work from its purer value as literature. The point Shea is compelled to make is that sociologically valuable subject matter does not make true poetry: She takes a stern reviewer's stance, as it were, against the kind of literary affirmative action that might unconscionably admit such writing into the Customs House of true poetry. Though Shea signals sensitivity to Halfe's cultural and racial context, she finally asserts that universal objective poetic standards must not be waived for racialized writers, lest they gain an unfair advantage in the courts of poetic adjudication. All citizens must stand equal before the law of Quality:

[T]he poet's language, while at times vibrant and precise, too often reads like prose rather than poetry. While Halfe's work clearly draws on an oral tradition (and might be better appreciated when read aloud), she subjects her poetic voices to the demands of the printed page. Judged by this standard, the subject matter of Blue Marrow *is more interesting than the infrequent flashes of poetry.*

Regardless of technical lapses, the author's emotional involvement and honesty cannot be questioned. Blue Marrow *makes a useful contribution to a fuller understanding of Canadian history.* (55)

In a similar vein, Deborah Jurdjevic appreciates the contribution Afua Cooper's *Memories Have Tongue* makes to anti-oppression struggles, but stops short – on a dime! – of admitting it as poetry: "*Memories Have Tongue* serves the need for a revisionist history in North America, particularly a history told by black women; it reclaims wordlessness with language" (108).

The material fact of the general division, however, is a crucial analytic for understanding Canadian poetry since the 1960s. To ignore or paper-over the divergence, to mollify the structural antagonisms, is to belittle poets' arguments and lives. Any scholar or reviewer who elides the division, by exclusive focus on one camp or the other, equally, writes a redactive, revisionary criticism.

The divided poetic field is a materially lived reality for Canadian poets, one struggled out in print culture, within the academy and outside. Which communities of readers? Which bookstores? Which anthologies? Which conferences? Which poets will be taught in which schools? Which magazines? Which coteries? Which festivals? Which reading venues? Which juries? Who will be interviewed by Evan Solomon? Who gets to perform in the Olympic Games opening ceremonies? Who gets to appear in a commercial for Nabob? Which poets will be allowed to teach writing? In what terms is the question 'what is poetry' posed? Or as John Hall asks: "What is the set of relationships implied by the act of writing?" (qtd. in Middleton, 129).

As the poetic differences keep spreading, the book reviews that publicly evaluate Canadian poetry (before and since the postmodern turn) continue to use an alarmingly consistent set of tropes, metaphors, concepts and rhetorical strategies. This critical lexicon, this ideolect, has its cultural ancestry in what Frank Davey identifies as an Arnoldian humanist criticism (in reference to the work of English Studies' supreme humanist-culturalist Matthew Arnold) combined with what Imre Szeman characterizes as Leavisite criticism, in reference to F.R. Leavis' institutional extension of the Arnoldian critical paradigm (Szeman 2001). Davey evokes Arnold in *Surviving the Paraphrase*, charging that:

Most of the weaknesses of thematic criticism stem from its origin in Arnoldian humanism, a tradition in which both the critic and the artist have a major responsibility to culture. In this view, the artist speaks, unconsciously or consciously, for the group. (Surviving 2)

More recently, Davey writes of the cultural views of former Governor General Adrienne Clarkson: "These views are mostly the romantic, nationalist, and Arnoldian humanist ones of the late nineteenth century, as elaborated by Leavis and Frye" (*Mr. and Mrs.* 146). Szeman writes more generally of the "the antipolitical universalism of Leavisite rhetoric" (613).

As Davey writes, again, in the Arnoldian critical paradigm inherited by Canadian critics, "[l]anguage ... is a tool employed not for its own intrinsic qualities but for the expression of ideas and visions" (*Surviving* 2). Furthermore, the "Arnoldian Ideal," as poet and critic E.D. Blodgett writes, orbits around "a predominant obsession ... with the idea of unity" (280-81). Blodgett continues:

In 'The Study of Poetry' Arnold cites The Imitation of Christ *to argue that no matter how much one reads or knows, it is necessary to return* 'ad unum ... principium' *which is 'the real' or 'the truly canonic'.* (281)

Robert Stacey adds to this picture of reviewers' ideolectic Arnoldianism. Reviewers often seek:

> what Matthew Arnold calls the 'high criticism of life' which, together with 'high seriousness', defines the 'classic character' of the truly great poets and distinguishes their work from the versifications of lesser minds. ("Toil" 69)

Unified form; the national voice and address; the great work of art as moral exemplar; supra-political, moral concepts of aesthetics; a paradigm of mimesis and expression; an essentially passive grasp of form; a fixation on judgement as the critic's duty; the need to identify the true article of cultural value; formal unity as signifying veracity: These are some of the basic assumptions, imperatives, and values of the Arnoldian-Leavisite ideolect dominant in Canadian poetry reviewing. (An "ideolect" is the language, dialect, of an ideology, distinct from "idiolect," which is a linguistic term for the idiomatic "linguistic system" of a single person.) Frederic Jameson expresses the bafflement of such a critic, who unexpectedly encounters the postmodern in poetry:

> If, indeed, the subject has lost its capacity actively to extend its pro-tensions and re-tensions across the temporal manifold and to organise its past and future into coherent experience, it becomes difficult enough to see how the cultural productions of such a subject could result in anything but 'heaps of fragments' and in a practice of the randomly heterogeneous and fragmentary and the aleatory. ("Postmodernism" 25)

In this mode of criticism, the mimetic verifiability of a poetic text, its immediate emotional intelligibility, and its capacity to communicate paraphraseable messages are taken as natural, concrete components of (what was once called) quality. The dominant underlying premise is expression: Poetic meaning is an expression of meanings that somehow exist prior to the poem. Consequently, form is often misconstrued as a mainly passive vessel.

The problem identified here marks the ideological division of the field of Canadian poetry: Postmodern poetry is predicated, programmatically, on rejecting or circumventing these inherited critical imperatives. Postmodern poetry is often directly antagonistic to the central demands made of poetry by that ideolect. To Davey, thematic criticism, the critical activities of paraphrase and the quest for the essential characteristics of a truly Canadian literature, misguided to start with, can say little about new poetry that aims, as far it can, to serve language rather than subject matter. While Davey's argument about language versus subject matter has often been reductively overplayed, its critical dictate remains cogent: New critical ideolects are needed to address new poetries. For this purpose, Davey envisions a textual criticism informed by transnational creative and critical influences, one that attempts to meet language at its material bases, and to meet poetry at the site of composition. A criticism of writerly concerns, embracing concepts drawn from cultural theory, Davey's is also a criticism of nervous response, an experiential and affective criticism of encounter with a text. What Davey envisions are *poetics*, rather than mercantile review criticism of imperative value judgement.

Postmodern poetry is less often reviewed than what might be called *perma*modern (in contrast to *post*modern) poetry, but not because of a readership differential. The dominant ideolect of Canadian poetry book reviews literally cannot conceive the concerns and questions engaged by postmodern poetries stemming from vanguard modernisms. Some of the ramifications of postmodern poetry contradict this ideolect too radically to (re)construct them as poetic values within that ideolect. Chiefly, postmodern poetry extends vanguard modernist poetry's project of linguistic rupture, fragmentation and formal innovation, with slim latent hopes or promises of mythic restoration. The contrast is sketched by Linda Hutcheon in the *Poetics of Postmodernism*:

Modernists like Eliot and Joyce have usually been seen as profoundly humanistic ... in their paradoxical desire for stable aesthetic and moral val-

ues, even in the face of their realization of the inevitable absence of such universals. Postmodernism differs from this, not in its humanistic contradictions, but in the provisionality of its response to them: it refuses to posit any structure or, what Lyotard ... calls, master narrative – such as art or myth – which, for such modernists, would have been consolatory. (6)

To many Canadian poetry reviewers, poetry takes a wrong turn somewhere, be it the late 19th century or in the early 1960s, somehow at once both into triviality and elitism.

A desire to return poetry to what reviewers fantasize it was before the cultural wrong turn at Albuquerque (or was it at Paterson?) is one of the constitutive drives of the dominant aesthetic conscience of Canadian poetry reviewing. Yet most reviewers are university-educated poets who have had direct exposure to contemporary critiques of dominant values. Furthermore, vernacular forms of concepts from critical theory are frequently found in the media contexts of entertainment journalism and in advertisements. Such ideas are not restricted to the discursive laboratories of academia. The ideas are out there. As Stanley Fish reminisces in his *New York Times* blog:

It was sometime in the '80s when I heard someone on the radio talking about Clint Eastwood's 1980 movie "Bronco Billy." It is, he said, a "nice little film in which Eastwood deconstructs his 'Dirty Harry' image.... [The term] had also been used with some precision.... If deconstruction was something that an American male icon performed, there was no reason to fear it; truth, reason and the American way were safe. ("French Theory")

The question to pose to reviewers is: If Derrida's ideas are good enough to write about the films of Clint Eastwood, why not about contemporary Canadian poetry?

An Idle Referendum

In his theory of the field of cultural production, Pierre Bourdieu charac-
terizes the modernist French art scene, constructing a useful analogue to
the Canadian poetic field:

*...schemes, which reproduce in their own logic the fundamental divisions
of the field of positions – 'pure art'/'commercial art,' 'bohemian'/'bourgeois',
'left bank'/'right bank', etc. – are one of the mediations through which dis-
positions are adjusted to positions. Writers and artists, particularly new-
comers, do not react to an 'objective reality' functioning as a sort of stim-
ulus valid for every possible subject, but to a 'problem-raising situation'.*
(1993: 64)

The "problem-raising situation" is the implicit or explicit question of po-
sition: Where do you stand? In Parisian theatre circles, it may be enough
to say such and such playwright is "left bank" to indicate his/her aesthet-
ic, moral, political position. In Canadian poetry, where the shorthand
is different, the rifts in Canadian poetry equally relieve many reviewers
of the task of textual critique. Reviews are used like signal lanterns in
the dark, to indicate relative position in the cultural field. That is to say,
reviews are often phatic, ritual gestures. The position-signal is often their
primary manifest content. As in Bourdieu's France, reliable position sig-
nals can be made with shorthand style tags. He is s an *experimental* poet.
She is a *postmodern* poet. He is a *lyric* poet. She is a *conceptual* poet. He
is a *confessional* poet. She is a *narrative* poet. He is an *experimental* poet.

She is a *KSW* (Kootenay School of Writing) poet. He is a *UVic* (University of Victoria) poet. She is a $L=A=N=G=U=A=G=E$ poet. He is a *spoken word* poet. She is a *feminist* poet. He is a *dub* poet. And so on. From such terms, other poets draw a range of positional inferences, valid or not, and base judgement and take discursive action on those inferences. Reviewers similarly use vernacular judgements of taste to make their guiding discriminations. Answers to evaluative queries – do you like [Canadian poet of prominence]'s work? – often tell other poets all they believe they need to know.

Between the function of phatic position-signals, and the expediency of using reductive judgements to send these signals, many reviewers simplify the duty of reviewing with an almost bureaucratic "model of standards-and-deviations" (Hernstein-Smith 1564). Evaluation and arbitration can entirely substitute for reading. In 1966, Roland Barthes already writes that:

The reader is ... plunged into a kind of idleness – he is intransitive; he is, in short, serious: instead of functioning himself, instead of gaining access to the magic of the signifier, to the pleasure of writing, he is left with no more than the poor freedom either to accept or reject the text: reading is nothing more than a referendum. (S/Z 4)

Strictly evaluative reviewing displaces the dynamic experience of reading for the experience of the polling booth (or ballot-box-office) – best figured in the star-ratings systems and "like" buttons on commercial websites. An idle referendum. In terms of aesthetic conscience, reviewers sometimes perform the role Hegel "picturesquely calls 'The Hard Heart' (*Das harte Herz*)" (Gram 327): One who seals him/herself behind the aquarium glass of his/her own categories, intellectually swimming in a vicious terminological circularity. The "judging consciousness [of the Hard Heart] ... repels [the] community of nature, and is the Hard Heart that is *for* itself, and which rejects any continuity with the other" (Hegel 405).

In Canada, a referendum model of the adjudicative review is natu-
ralized in reviewers' ideolect as the "proper business of criticism" – the
duty-imperative animating reviewers' aesthetic consciences. As reviewer
James Wood says in an interview with Lorna Jackson:

I think the more meaningful distinction, nowadays, is between critic and
academic. The critic, in my sense of the word, lives by the pen, prosecutes
arguments, devotes his life to the examination of literature, works in the
public realm (i.e., magazines and newspapers), writes for the common
reader (that frail, tenacious plant), and is above all intensely interested in
value judgement, in deciding whether something is good or bad. (110)

Wood's characterization of the critic in his "sense of the word" dem-
onstrates how cultural field positions are defined relationally. He first
marks the line of discrimination between the "critic and academic" as
the most important. All that follows defines both positions: One (the
critic) positively, the other (academic) negatively. The characteristics as-
cribed to the critic are precisely those the academic does not exhibit, and
vice versa. Behind his construction of both positions is the Ivory Tower
trope, the fantasy notion that academics, and the site of a fantasy Aca-
demia, are removed from (something called) real life. Academia is clois-
tered, academics are pasty-faced shut-ins out of touch with the blood-
and-guts truth of everyday struggle. Hence Wood's initial clause, which
constructs the critic as a romantic swashbuckler who lives (and dies,
presumably) by the pen-sword. Mercenary, musketeer, swollen with pas-
sionate vitality, this critic lives in the fray of the common crowd, down
in the smelly, competitive reality of the marketplace. Real life, the world,
Wood believes, happens in commerce, in "magazines and newspapers."
His final flourish about judgement as the master imperative makes the
stakes of the game, as it were, those of life and death. The referendum he
holds over a book is staged as a duel.

Although many Canadian poetry reviews are putatively descriptive rather than evaluative, like plot summaries of poetic devices or charts of the curve of quality, the dominant imperative in these reviews remains evaluative. In strongly adjudicative book reviews, consumer intent is passive-aggressively articulated in terms of "audience expectations," expectations projected out of the reviewer's aesthetic conscience. Consistent with an underlying economism, that centres authenticity in sites of commerce (the marketplace, the market, etc.), poetry here exists to serve a pre-existent set of tastes, needs, demands, expectations, rather than iteratively producing such needs – its public – through a dialogical process. Pauline Butling, against this grain, argues in favour of a specific iteration of postmodern poetry:

My *postmodernism was as much a liberatory and community-building project as a set of formally innovative practices.... [P]ostmodern poets intentionally developed oppositional sites ... they produced a 'counterpublic' comprised of new readers and writers who championed various 'locals.'* (315)

When challenged by new poetry, reviewers like Wood behave like angry customers: Why doesn't this poet give me what I desire? I ordered the empathy steak, not the scrambled subjectivity. Instead of the better questions: What does this poet do and how can I address it? As Barbara Hernstein Smith argues in "The Contingency of Value:"

Thus it will be assumed or maintained ... that the particular functions [reviewers] expect and desire the class of objects in question (for example, "works of art" or "literature") to perform are their intrinsic or proper functions, all other expected, desired or emergent functions being inappropriate, irrelevant, extrinsic, abuses of the true nature of those objects or violations of their authorially intended or generically intrinsic purposes. (1566)

The former question sets up a collision of monologues. The latter question opens itself to the dialogic modes of reader-writer-reader relationships formally proposed in postmodern poetry.

Dominant categories of poetic value, drawn from the Arnoldian-Leavisite set, provide the dominant aesthetic conscience of Canadian poetry reviewing with its ideolect. The specificity of an ideolect – the narrowness of its categories – is constructed as rigour, its contingent value-constructions as discoveries of aesthetic fact. The ideolect comes increasingly to seem to be the correct language of poetry criticism, as if its values are ones it discovers rather than ones it inscribes. These effects are part of the process of aesthetic conscience, which works to confirm the validity of its own constitutive categories by projecting them as universals. To Immanuel Kant, the primary dictum of conscience is the question: "Can I will that the maxim on which I am prepared to act become universal law?" (qtd. in Despland 358). Reviewers' terminal judgements are often bound to their answers to speculative universalizations: "What if all poets were to write this way?" Or: "Where would the influence of such poetry lead our poetic youth?" For the universalizing aesthetic question of conscience to be coherent, the categories which generate it must themselves have general or universal validity – there must be a discoverable ground of objectivity on which to base judgement. The dominant reviewers' ideolect is therefore projected as a timeless code, above critique.

Unified Global Voice

Postmodern poetry is both experiential and meta-experiential; it both produces visceral experience, and overtly frames experience as experience. Not that postmodernity produces the first self-reflective events in literary history, by any means. As Robert Stacey writes in his introduction to *Re: Reading the Postmodern*:

[T]he 'postmodernity' of a text is ... a question of the disposition of these elements [intertextuality, self-reflexivity, irony, parody, indeterminacy, aleatory] and how they are marked by and 'carry over' the new social content of which they are the translation. The same things, in other words, have different meanings (now). The difference is history.... (xxvi)

When it makes these factors, and this historical shift, difficult, if not impossible, to recognize and validate, the dominant ideolect of the Canadian poetry review makes postmodern poetry (almost) literally unreadable. The spurious accusation of illegibility (categorically spurious, because no text is illegible and anything can be read as a text) levelled at postmodern poetry is thus structurally predictable, a discursive position-taking predicated on antagonisms constitutive of the poetic field. As Bourdieu writes:

by endeavouring to impose new modes of thought and expression, out of key with the prevailing modes of thought and with the doxa, [new poetics are] therefore bound to disconcert the orthodox by their 'obscurity' and 'pointlessness.' (*Field* 58)

31

Recall Fredric Jameson's readings of postmodern texts and artworks in "Postmodernism, or, The Cultural Logic of Late Capitalism." Although he identifies paratactic literature with a schizophrenic condition of late capitalism (as per Lacan), "when the links in the signifying chain snap" (26), Jameson stoops a moment to read Bob Perelman's poem "China" sympathetically. Jameson's account of "China" tells much more about the critical categories (and attendant conventions) postmodern poetry violates than his oddly literal thesis tells about the poem:

Many things could be said about this interesting exercise in discontinuities; not the least paradoxical is the re-emergence here across these disjointed sentences of some more unified global meaning. Indeed, insofar as this is in some curious and secret way a political poem, it does seem to capture something of the excitement of the immense, unfinished social experiment of the New China ... the freshness of a whole new object world produced by human beings in control of their collective destiny ... the collectivity ... after the long subjugation of feudalism and imperialism, again speaks its own voice, for itself, as though for the first time. (29)

A number of assumptions about meaning and textuality govern Jameson's interpretation. Most essential are his mimetic and expressive assumptions about meaning. A text represents and/or expresses its meaning, it does not perform or constitute its meaning. The imperative of a text must finally be to create a paraphrasable sense or a representation of something other than itself. To such reading, the "disjointed" components of a text like Perelman's can only ever be pieces of a puzzle. Reassembly becomes the test of the critic's competence, he/she has to either find the unity hidden by "discontinuity," walk away defeated or declare the work not true poetry. No mind as powerful as Jameson's is going to be defeated, so he is bound to find exactly the unity he does find. Rather than shift his reading to another register, he discovers the "re-emergence ... of some more unified global meaning" that resolves, no less, into the subjectivist trope of vocality. He reassembles the puzzle. Perelman's poem, thus resurrected by the critic, "again speaks its own voice" in expression and mimesis together.

Contrast Perelman's explication of the poem in his response to Jameson's reading:

I should remark here that the rhetorical tone of "China" [is] one of the basic features of the poem.... [T]he poem touches on matter-of-fact utopian feelings that early education can evoke. The opening line ... combines rudimentary astronomy with an assertion of complete independence, as if learning about the solar system in second grade marks a liberation from older narratives of fate.... The same tension appears in a line such as: "Everyone enjoyed the explosions." It means one thing if 'everyone' refers to a rural village celebrating the new year with firecrackers ... but if the context is the Vietnam War, the meaning changes: the explosions now are deadly, and 'everyone' loses its utopic-communal character, becoming a designation that embodies colonialist repression. ("New Sentence" 322-323)

Perelman nowhere mentions mimesis or expression as a compositional factor. Instead, like many postmodern poems, "China" is built on the very ambiguities in language that make language so serviceable for ideology. The poet activates polysemy on the formal level by parataxis, and activates it contextually with indexical signs. "China," as Perelman spells out above, is hardly a neutral word. Its amusingly "matter-of-fact" tone further underlines the availability of each fragment to reaccentuation or reinscription by rival interests. In particular, terms like "everyone" and "explosions" are radically different, depending on who speaks or reads them. In the instantaneity of poetic synthesis, a reader can experience all these rival ascriptions at once. No mimetic puzzle to solve, no global unity to discover. "China" like so many poems is a *mise-en-scène* of ideology in discourse, it allows a reader to see vectors of the linguistic, social and historical cross within the event of the poem, to glimpse for a moment the dialogic social truth of language which ideology (necessarily) obscures.

Michael Davidson characterizes the contrast between modern and postmodern poetics somewhat differently:

Whereas for modernists the defamiliarisation of words implies a desire for a realm of pure literariness, for Language-writers defamiliarisation involves the interrogation of discursive and ideological structures. (qtd. in Derksen 51)

Postmodern poetry works, as far as it can, to foreground the operations of representation and/or linguistic subject-formation in and through poetry as it happens. The very constructedness of the poem is a thematic concern, a poetry that tries to teach itself the trick of watching itself watching and being watched. Writing at the site of writing. The act of composition. The time and memory-bound contingencies of textual verisimilitude. Writing's productive and reproductive mechanisms (typewriter, page, voice, codex, keyboard, screen, etc.). The community relations through which a notion of the poetic takes shape. Contingencies of value. Contingencies of meaning. This in contrast with humanist poetry of Big Affect (in the tradition of what Ron Silliman hilariously, although too globally, calls the "School of Quietude") that aligns trajectories of representation, rhetoric, and imperative towards identifiable ends of expression, emotion, morality, and mimesis. The poetry of subjective voice, unity, closure, and aesthetic rapture, the very poetry Jameson pretends to excavate from beneath Perelman's "heaps of fragments."

Quasi-Mechanical

Bruce Serafin's hard-hearted review (in *Books in Canada*) of Steve Mc-Caffery's critical book *North of Intention* provoked a memorable confrontation in the ongoing positions war within Canadian poetry. Although Serafin, author of the books *Colin's Big Thing* and *Stardust*, often reveals in his other writings a complex, perhaps postmodern, sensibility, when set to the task of reviewing the most normative imperatives of his aesthetic conscience take control. The result is almost a *foie gras* of The-Best-and-the-Beautiful culturism, categorically incompatible with the counter-individualist, para-institutional practices in postmodern poetry.

Not incidentally, McCaffery's rebuttal presents evidence that Serafin never actually read *North of Intention*. Serafin didn't need to read *North of Intention*. The type of position-taking, and phatic position-signal he performs, requires no textual critique; it only has to go so far as to discover a terminological incompatibility. The position he constructs for McCaffery is based on the phantasm of the malign Academy; it has little to do with specific arguments about propositional content. Serafin only has to report on the type of discourse he imagines he finds, and articulate his own position antagonistically. From the perspective of Bourdieu's model of the cultural field, this is because:

[P]osition-takings arise quasi-mechanically – that is, almost independently of the agents' consciousness and wills – from the relationship between positions, they take relatively invariant forms, and being determined ra-

tionally, negatively, they may remain virtually empty, amounting to little
more than a parti pris *of refusal, difference, rupture.* (*Field* 61)

Serafin's review, entitled "Colonial Mentalities" (echoing Robin
Mathews), first attributes McCaffery's methodology to a colonial inferi-
ority complex, then moves into a more positional argument. He decides
that:

the problem is that McCaffery is bringing a scholarly type of criticism to
bear on writers whose interest lies chiefly in their eccentricity. By "schol-
arly" I mean the kind of work usually found in academic articles on Kafka
or Blake or William Congreve – i.e., articles that take the literary worth of
their authors for granted and subject them to little or no evaluation, being
interested instead in some aspect of what they have done. Now, by treating
his writers this way McCaffery is making a claim about them: he is imply-
ing that their literary worth is in some sense indisputable. ("Colonial")

(Did Serafin fail to notice the canonization of Gertrude Stein, Ezra
Pound, James Joyce and Samuel Beckett?) The core stake here, out of
which Serafin constructs the differential positions of the bodiless aca-
demic versus the bare-knuckle reviewer, is how each type values the
problem of value itself. As Serafin has it, there might not be an argument
if he agreed with (what he takes as) McCaffery's implicit appraisals of
the writers, or if academic consecration had made their value "indisput-
able." He also assumes that McCaffery shares his own evaluative impera-
tive (even if he hides his value claims), so Serafin's attack hinges on the
counter-evaluation of the writers McCaffery discusses: They are inter-
esting "chiefly for their eccentricity." (Notwithstanding that by 1990, the
year Serafin's review is published, postmodern poetry is a large enough
movement that such "eccentricity" is already a well-established counter
tradition or parallel tradition to official verse culture.) What character-
izes the "scholarly type" of criticism for Serafin – what's really at stake

in the difference between positions he defines – is not methodology per se, but whether judgement is the imperative and goal. To Serafin, judgement-driven reviewing is of the people, in the fray of strugglesome real life, versus the bloodless aloofness to value of aristocratic academic criticism.

What Serafin objects to in McCaffery's critical practice is exactly what Davey calls for – criticism at the site of writing, or *poetics* – which entails a redefinition of the role of both the practical critic and the academic critic, driven by imperatives other than judgement. The value referendum is absolutely not the only reason to review a new book, nor the only way to review a new book, nor the only reason, broadly, to be attentive to and give column inches to discussion of contemporary writing. Serafin's attitude to Academia, however, is more ambivalent than James Wood's above. For Serafin (a writer afforded a lot of street-cred), the prestigious attention of a disinterested poetics is reserved only for authors already sanctioned by English departments – places he seems to assume operate under value consensus. Academia is one of the recurrent tropes of fantasy in this ideolect, an alien place, treated by antagonists as a determinate, unitary position in the poetic field (hence the often pejorative term: "poet-professor"). So Serafin at once reviles the "academic" language McCaffery uses as "corporate," yet grants only that same academia the power to consecrate contemporary writers like himself. Although Serafin rejects academicism, as Davey accused Robert Lecker: "[He] seems to know of only one constructor of literary canons – a unitary academy" (656). In the name of a phantasmic Common Reader, Serafin's discourse disempowers living writers and concrete literary communities.

The following passage is a major juncture in Serafin's argument, the point at which he shifts drastically away from consideration of the book itself, to use it instead as token of an historical symptom.

So a paradox arises: seeking the largest language, the language that seems most international, most part of an over-arching intellectual project, the critic ends up writing for fewer and fewer people. Wanting to be significant, he first of all loses his "place," then his sense of proportion, his ease with his native speech, and finally his pleasure in the use of language. The loss of speech: one keeps coming back to that. ("Colonial")

In other words: this is your brain on postmodernism. The living person is diagnostically shamed, while others are warned away from his/her disordered path. The reviewer's position in the field is thus affirmatively signalled, so others may rally to that position, either for the first time or in ritual re-affirmation. Serafin's critique, however, is premised mainly in the question of value. He does not warn so much against inflated cultural ambitions as mark "internationalism" and "over-arching" positions as illicit. (Note that this clashes with the idiosyncratic set of names he uses to construct Tradition: Blake + Kafka + Congreve.) The loss of a "sense of proportion" is a loss of correct guiding values. "Place" is framed in scare quotes to activate a polysemy that suggests McCaffery is intellectually lost, and that he has forfeited his rightful social place. He hasn't merely lost "speech," he has forfeited the gift of inherited "native speech" – which is to say inherited cultural categories of value. The unsubtly xenophobic implication is that, by working from international (here French) sources, McCaffery renounces both his cultural citizenship and his humanity. McCaffery becomes a speechless foreigner (what are those strange sounds he makes?), an alien (without human empathy, unrecognizable).

Treason, Humanism, Diaspora

Why postmodern poetry causes a flashpoint in the national cultural project, both in terms of the types of books written, and how they are reviewed, can be gleaned from studies by E.D. Blodgett, Frank Davey and Linda Hutcheon of the postmodern in Canadian literature.

1 The new writing is influenced from elsewhere (usa and France), aggravating in some reviewers what Northrop Frye called Canadians' "garrison mentality," which intensifies the fetish of a demonstrably "Canadian" poetry.
2 The new writing is antithetical to the inherited ideolect and ideology, antithetical to core received notions and values in Canadian literature. Questions of cultural identity in the representation of society and landscape, the valuation of unity and critical imperative of judgement, are problematized in postmodern poetry rather than affirmed.
3 The new writing (therefore) requires reviewers to address it with new critical ideolects.

Notable is the new emphasis on *writing*, foregrounded against either the phantasm of the writer (on which reviewers can hang the toga of literary celebrity), or the phantom of a national cultural project. Postmodern texts generally invert, as Barthes proposed, the emphasis of writer versus reader. Where thematic, mimetic, intentionalist modes of criticism falsely construct the critic as a virtuosic customer-detective of meanings, postmodern writing emphasizes, on multiple registers, that any reader is

always already an active co-producer of a text. Despite Barthes' charac-
terisation of this shift of emphasis in terms of play, or a quasi-orgasmic
jouissance, the inversion of roles arguably creates new responsibilities for
reviewers and critics. Without recourse to simplistic formulae of value
(as quality), their responsibilities are more difficult than before. Rather
than testing new writings against preformulated standards, critical prac-
tice becomes a matter of finding the critical ideolect, or set of method-
ologies, commensurate to a given text. As Hernstein Smith writes:

[T]he conceptual structures and methodological practices adopted ...
would themselves be historically and otherwise contingent ... their specific
value as descriptions and accounts would be a function of how well they
made intelligible the phenomena within their domain to whoever, at whut-
ever time and from whatever perspective, had an interest in them. (1560)

Such shifts are not easy to make, and become harder to make the more
competence a critic acquires in a given ideolect. The more expert the
critic is in a specific reading methodology – such as the judgement-driv-
en Canadian poetry book review – the harder the shift is to make.

I propose that the history of poetry reviewing in Canada since 1961
divides into three major phases – roughly: 1961–1978; 1974–1995; 1994
onwards. A fourth phase may have begun sometime around the Chris-
tian Bök versus Carmine Starnino debate at Mount Royal University in
2009. If so, the new period remains emergent. Furthermore, my provi-
sional periodization only accounts for continuities and shifts within a
dominant, not for important interventions against this dominant.

As stated, I mark the start of the first phase with John R. Colombo's
1961 review in *The Canadian Forum* of *Tish* and *Cataract*, not because
Colombo's review has had influence I've been able to discern, but be-
cause the date of its publication is a good benchmark of the process
through which postmodern poetry becomes a topic of national literary
debate. Colombo dismisses the poetics of *Tish* (and any foreign influ-

ence) as stale, imported goods: "all of Canada's cultural revolutions have been imported, abortive, and a bit late" (212). His review thus signals the complication and expansion of the positions struggles that redefine (and multiply divide) the poetic field in Canada. In the wake of George Grant's *Lament for a Nation*, reviewers like Robin Mathews (more professedly Marxist than Frank Davey, yes, but a far less sophisticated theorist of discourse and power), George Woodcock (an anarchist, yes, but a simplistic, normative poetry reviewer) and W.H. New (among the founders of postcolonial studies in Canada, yes, but as a poetry reviewer, an enthusiastic member of the dominant evaluative community) resort to a form of cultural protectionism in journals and magazines such as *Canadian Literature* (1959), *Canadian Notes & Queries* (1968) and *Books in Canada* (1972), sometimes with outright accusations of cultural treason. In the very same phase, other reviewers, anti-nationalists like Mordecai Richler, openly wonder if there even is any "Canadian culture" worth protecting. This divisive phase arguably culminates with the publication of two books: *Poetry and the Colonized Mind: Tish* (1976) by Keith Richardson, and Mathews' *Canadian Literature: Surrender or Revolution* (1978) which reiterate an opposition to USAmerican "cultural imperialism" (Mathews) first articulated in book reviews.

I mark the second phase in 1974. In this year, Robert Kroetsch declares (erroneously, I believe) that Canadian literature "evolved directly from Victorian to Postmodern," just when the first translation of Roland Barthes' highly influential *S/Z* reaches Anglophone Canada. The date/location of the first appearance of the term postmodern in Canadian print is periodically revised. Kroetsch is correctly credited with bringing the term forward in 1974, but it is already in circulation among academics before that date. Frank Davey uses it earlier in an interview that Robin Blaser quotes in the introduction to *Particular Accidents* (Blaser 29), and in 1974 uses the term in *From There to Here* (19-21). Robert Stacey further shows how the term is contested from the start, and adds to its lore:

That same year [1974] likely marks the date of the earliest appearances of the word 'postmodern' in Canadian print, in at least two sources: Davey's From There to Here, *where it signalled the advent of a new age of decentralized and dispersed power and its concomitant aesthetics of 'process, discontinuity, and organic shape' … and Douglas Barbour's 'Down With History: Some Notes Towards an Understanding of Beautiful Losers,' where it referred to the anti-logic of libidinal excess, stylistic promiscuity, and narrative interference at work in Cohen's novel.* ("Introduction" xv-xvi)

Regardless, Barthes' postmodern *S/Z* is indeed among the first books in a wave of theoretical writings arriving from France. Although poststructuralist concepts have been current in academia since the mid-1960s, with translations of books like *S/Z* the powerful critical tools of French poststructuralist theory fall into the hot hands of many more Anglophone Canadian poets. As the project of national literary identity gains momentum, other (anti-essentialist) impulses are felt from the direction of cultural studies. Between the two, poets feel forced to re-imagine the cultural role, and importance, of their art. These multiple, complex pressures create a new class of poet-critics, highly articulate in defence of their work (and that of others), whose ideas, disseminated widely among Canadian poets, pose a deep threat to the mystical, conscientious authority of the Leavisite poetry judge. These influential figures include, by year of first-book publication: George Bowering (1963), Frank Davey (1965), Fred Wah (1965), bpNichol (1967), Daphne Marlatt (1968), Steve McCaffery (1974), Robert Kroetsch (1976; first book of poetry), Roy Miki (1976), Erín Moure (1979), Gail Scott (1981), Margaret Christakos (1988), Jeff Derksen (1991), Lisa Robertson (1993), Nancy Shaw (1993), Christian Bök (1994), Darren Wershler (1997), Stephen Cain (1999), Sina Queyras (2001), and Roger Farr (2006).

With such adversaries, reviewers in journals like *Canadian Poetry* (1977), *Poetry Canada Review* (1979) and *The Vancouver Review* (1989) shift the accent from either cultural protectionism or cultural self-hate towards aesthetic and "humanist" concerns. In a process further encouraged by cultural globalization and the advances of neoliberalism, the universal customer and the universal human subject become conflated. Typically, reviewers like Brian Fawcett, Bruce Serafin and Greg Gatenby attack poetry that appears theory-savvy (whether or not the poets are affiliated with academia) as anti-social, or incomprehensible, and with pseudo-populist soothsaying. As Brian Fawcett writes in a review of the 1989 anthology *East of Main*: "LCW [Language-Centred Writing] is … interesting enough as a theoretical principle, but its uncommunicativeness makes it of dubious value as a long-term practice" ("East Van" 101). One might ask at what point the communicative content of a poetics becomes a measure of, or equivalent to, its canonic value. Fawcett knows as well as any critic that poetry isn't just an effect of artfully saying what you mean, but he essentially makes that argument here in his drive to mute the socio-political implications of postmodern poetry.[1] Although many such reviewers identify publicly as Leftist, their critical imperative is often to discredit the strong political inclinations of postmodern poetry, and to discredit cultural theory as a discourse alien to poetry. Value-normative, counter-political poetry reviewing, even by a reviewer who self-identifies as Leftist, remains politically reactionary, if not Rightist in its ramifications. In particular, investigations of the premise that "everything is political" (such an important conceptual dimension of postmodern poetry) provoke dread wherever they open into features of art beyond paraphraseable "political" content.

I mark the third, (still current?) phase at 1994. Although Microsoft releases the first version of Windows in 1985, it is not until the mid-90s that internet and cheap desktop publishing become commonplace

---

1   With hindsight, his concern about loss of audience is contrary to lived experience; he makes his forecast at the very same moment that the Canadian postmodern poetry is building significant local and international publics for Canadian poetry.

enough to reshape the Canadian literary field. (In 1993, for example, Peter Mansbridge hosts a C B C special about "A Computer Network Called Internet." He declares that, "The internet is no longer just for nerds.") From that time, along with repeated challenges to the possibility of any singular Canadian literary canon, the pluralization of poetic practices increases so exponentially that any reviewer's (already tenuous) claim to authoritative centrality is fatally dispersed.

Today, "Canadian poetry" encompasses such a variety of complimentary, contradictory and antagonistic practices that Canadian poetry cannot be defined by reference to style, form, content, theme, tone, manner, aesthetic values or provenance. As confessed, the particular discursive struggles I examine here, between the ideolects of post- and perma-modern poetries, do not account for the even greater diversity of the poetic field. This diversification is a positive development. It is only good for Canadian poetry. If the writings of Ken Rivard (*Kiss Me Down to Size*), Wendy Morton (*Private Eye*), Darren Wershler (*The Tapeworm Foundry*), jwcurry (*Objectionable Perspectives*), Gustave Morin (*The Etc Bbq*), Lillian Allen (*Women Do This Everyday*) and Afua Cooper (*Memories Have Tongue*) all count as Canadian poetry (and they certainly do all count), its only possible definition is as a Duchampian tautology. Canadian poetry is cultural product identified by readers of Canadian poetry as Canadian poetry. Any other type of definition must be – contrary to the actual plurality of practices – prescriptive, proscriptive and normative. Any criticism that searches for an authentic Canadian literature is violently essentialist and historically redactive.

This pluralization of practices, and consequent dispersal of critical authority, produces in some territories a predictable (from the perspective of field positions and aesthetic conscience) outbreak of reactionary phobia. Some reviewers react as if to admit the contingency of poetic value would trigger a cataclysm, as if the poetic field cannot survive its modification by the entry of new (rival) modes of value. Consequently, what Charles Altieri calls "neo-pragmatism" arises. Arch-conservative reviewers like Carmine Starnino, Shane Neilson, Zachariah Wells, Robyn Sarah, Alex Good, David Ormsby, Michael Lista and David Solway (among others) campaign in print and in online venues, such as *The Danforth Review* (1999) and *Maisonneuve* (2002) and the *National Post* (1998), to reduce the terms of review-criticism to a quantifiable set of values that define "real" Canadian poetry: what Hernstein-Smith calls "model of standards-and-deviations" criticism. After predecessors like Greg Gatenby, J.K. Snyder, Bruce Serafin, Rosemary Aubert, and Patrick Lane, these Common Sense Police write reviews that come as close to ideological lockdown as possible. As Hernstein-Smith predicts, they meet the awareness of contingency with violently blunt, defensive assertions of noncontingency:

Consequently, institutions of evaluative authority [are] called upon repeatedly to devise arguments and procedures that validate the community's established tastes and preferences, thereby warding off barbarism and the constant apparition of an imminent collapse of standards and also justifying their own normative authority. (1565)

Adjudicative reviewers attempt to apply a pseudo-empirical, naked positivism to the abstract, insubstantial matter of poetry. At its purest, such hard-hearted aesthetic conscience works to formulate the quality of a poem as a set of quantities that can be tallied – fundamentalists of the aesthetic god-trope Quality.

To Further a Deliberate Whole

Poetry reviewing as practiced in Canada, the whole foundation if not the edifice of Canada's practical criticism, is categorically challenged by postmodern poetry. The shift proposed, by example, is away from any notion of Quality as such, towards an expanded concept of poetic value. Quality is not a material given in the poem or on the page. Quality is only an interim name for the affiliative effects of collaboratively constructed valuation and belief. After critiques of realist aesthetics, and with postmodern poetry's valuation of the microscopically local, reviewers are burdened with the knowledge that value is locally contingent, which obliterates the reassuring futurity of hope that one day the non-social objective (lawful) bases of aesthetic Quality will be found. Poetic (aesthetic) value is a complex social construction that arises only partially from a person's direct interaction with a particular sequence of words. Words on the page are very little in-and-of-themselves. As Peter Middleton writes of postmodern poetry:

Almost all readers can perceive that these innovative poems immediately incite a question: Is this really a poem? A consequent dismissal of the alleged pretender often follows from a failure to recognise that this question cannot be limited to a reified set of linguistic marks on sheets of paper. A poem is complexly extended through history, and therefore in space, time and subjectivity, in ways that are an intrinsic part of its being as a poem. Its meaning takes place during a multiplicity of temporally and spatially organised occasions. (128-129)

The issue I raise here about critical language and literary ideology in reviews cuts across the CanLit demilitarized (dematerialized?) zones. Many poets in the trajectory of the postmodern write reviews in the same ideolect as their concrete antagonists. In these cases, the reviewers are forced to find ways to valuate postmodern poetry through categories it functionally opposes. (Again: In analyzing these specific book reviews, I rarely make claims about reviewers' other writings, and never attack anyone personally.) When rob mclennan, for example, who has published more than 20 books of poetry, praises his stylistic mentor Barry McKinnon, he writes in the dominant ideolect of the Canadian poetry review:

Working in the poetic tradition of the procedural open-form, Barry McKinnon's poetry is finely tuned and honed, where the craft is there, but it is the movement that represents.... It's as though McKinnon works through a deliberate incompletion, moving and moving further out in each piece until there is nowhere else for him to go, writing lines precisely cut to further a deliberate whole. ("The Centre")

Note the altered sense of tradition here, in a postmodern 2004. mclennan's tradition and McKinnon's tradition, versus Bruce Serafin's tradition, is a tradition of formal non-unity, of rupture; postmodern poetry's "procedural open form." In this strain of postmodern poetry, the younger poet mclennan is not engaged in intergenerational struggle with his mentor. Yes, the poetic field in Canada splits into multiple traditions, and multiple incompatible readings of history, whether or not official verse culture has the ideological capacity to see this actual, combative plurality, as anything more than a tokenistic, notional diversity.

Writing about a poet he has studied and emulated, mclennan's sentence introduces at least five of the major tropes basic to the dominant ideolect of Canadian poetry book reviews: work, tradition, craftsmanship, poem-as-object, unity. The "procedural open-form" of McKinnon's poetry (not to mention mclennan's own) contradicts or problematizes, if not nullifies, most of mclennan's terms of praise. Yet to validate for a phantasmic Common Reader the "deliberate incompletion" of McKinnon's poetry, mclennan frames it as projected towards a greater unity. That is what he means by the phrase "to further a deliberate whole." As with Jameson's reading of "China," this is a mimesis of writerly subject and textual form, the excavation of a unity beneath the fragmentary: Barry McKinnon, the Man-Poem. With this concept of "greater unity" mclennan overemphasizes the sense of persona operant in McKinnon's work, and returns to altar of formal Unity: "ad unum ... principium." mclennan categorically eviscerates in ideological ritual what he would celebrate. Another crucial marker is the difficulty mclennan has articulating his grasp of form as actively constitutive of meaning. The strain in mclennan's sentence, "it is the movement that represents," is that of a widely published, highly accomplished postmodern poet of "procedural open-form" trying to read such form critically. The dominant review ideolect provides him with no means to read form dialogically. Northrop Frye, writing in 1961, deals with the form-content problem with greater acuity than this experienced postmodern poet and critic. Frye notes how the "irony of form" presents a basic interpretative problem to any critic: "the literary structure is always ironic because 'what it says' is always different from 'what it means'" (qtd. in Davey 3)[2].

U S A merican poet-critic Juliana Spahr, as she works towards new modes of reading in "Everybody's Autonomy," produces a similarly passive formulation:

To ignore the formal characteristics of the work is to ignore one of the crucial ways works carry meaning. Further, such an approach reads all work as bland and apolitical. (12)

---

2 This is to not at all to unfairly compare mclennan's erudition against Northrop Frye's, only to emphasize a case where yet another postmodern practitioner discursively chokes his ability to articulate even what *his own* poetry does.

To say that form can "carry meaning" is not pointed enough, not now or ever. Her syntax here makes the statement read as if she means: Form *also* has meaning. Many reviewers' inability to read form dialogically, and inability to read contextual choices at the macro level of poetics and culture, demonstrates that the ideolect of the Canadian poetry review still constructs form as a neutral container, well-wrought or not so well-wrought, of message contents. In this sense, the critical ideolect of Canadian poetry book reviews has not even minimally kept up with many poetic practices initiated over 50 years ago. In his defence of Christian Bök's *Eunoia*, Robert Stacey emphasizes the need to read form if works in the poetic postmodern stream are to be critically intelligible. He writes that: "Eunoia really does express something meaningful, even important, but only to the degree that we listen to what its organizing principle and its resultant form ... have to say" ("Toil" 69).

Juliana Spahr's second sentence above is noteworthy in this light. In the ideological framework of the Canadian poetry review, there is often a predictable retreat into the assumption that only manifest, paraphraseable content of a text has political valence – neither a text's formal properties nor cultural positioning can have legible political meaning. The social complexity of the political in these schemata is collapsed into a paradigm of policy debate and pseudo-democratic process. Neither form nor context can emerge as actively meaningful, so reviewers often cannot educe broader implications from formal or contextual decisions that are crucial to the compositional strategies of postmodern poetry. As Peter Middleton regrets:

Discourses of current poetics in the U.K. have foundered on these difficulties, which are made worse by what Jeff Derksen calls the lack of method for tracing connections between poetic forms and social praxis. Poetry has often been more inventive than the public discourses that have promulgated it. (136)

Sound of the Police

As Prime Minister Stephen Harper has said, conservative values are Canadian values. The tendency in Canadian poetry reviewing towards what Lawrence Grossberg calls the quasi-positivist "assumption that there is only one valid way of knowing" (128) has accelerated since the early 1960s, when the postmodern troubles began. Consider, for example, Al Purdy – a poet often upheld as a secular saint of middlebrow, masculinist, beer-based poetry for Average Joe Canada – reviewing Roy Kiyooka's *Kyoto Airs* in a round-up review of books by John Newlove, Gerry Gilbert and Roy Kiyooka in *The Canadian Forum* in 1964:

Roy Kiyooka is a slightly-other kettle of idiom … [Kiyooka] certainly has cut away extraneous material and verbiage from his writing. In a remarkable poem called 'The Warrior', Kiyooka creates an energy vortex in which all things turn inward and circle to an end inside the poem without question. The poem answers any implicit questions in process of asking. (143)

Contrast this with Shane Neilson, author of three books of poetry and former poetry editor at *The Danforth Review*, reviewing Roy Miki's *Surrender* in 2002, as part of a five-part suite of reviews treating all the poetry titles nominated for the Governor General's Award that year.

In this book, it is difficult to pick just one offence against style and taste; Surrender *is instead a repeat offender…. Indeed, confusion's a constitutive experience when reading through the whole book. But I must ask: who wanders on a tarmac desiring insularity...? In Canada, he had no reason to be intelligible, he was rewarded precisely for being unintelligible....* Surrender *is anti-poetry; it deserved no award, and that it won the GG suggests the irrelevance of the institution.* ("*Surrender*")

Al Purdy, back in 1964, has a more individualized yet open aesthetic conscience than Neilson. He is not nearly as bound by the dominant review ideolect as Neilson. Purdy is careful to register the quality of Kiyooka's poetry, first of all, with familiar crafts discourse. Kiyooka, like a good carver or a good butcher, has chopped and cut away "extraneous material and verbiage," like waste marble or chicken fat. Yet Purdy is immediately comfortable with Kiyooka's poetry as a poetry of difference, an idiosyncratic "kettle of idiom" that behaves in unexpected ways. He does not, therefore, read Kiyooka's poetry through an evaluative checklist of standards and deviations based on categories of mimetic verifiability, immediate emotional legibility, and capacity to communicate messages – because such standards do not reflect the values inferable from the poetry. Using only his own sensitivity and verbal ingenuity, without academic training in cultural theory, Purdy is perfectly able to read the effects of the form of Kiyooka's poetry. Furthermore, Purdy's review does not construct form as a passive container of content. To Purdy, Kiyooka's formal decisions "answer any implicit questions" they are as meaningful as whatever direct message-content the poem purports. He even lays down a compelling sentence of vernacular, poetic theory in his description of those effects: "Kiyooka creates an energy vortex in which all things turn inward and circle to an end inside the poem without question." Whether or not Kiyooka's poetry makes it through the checkpoints of immanent Quality, Purdy has had a complex experience that he relates without strain. Whatever his tastes dictate, Purdy knows that no text is illegible.

Shane Neilson's review, by contrast, is a stinging swarm of the dominant poetic value categories. Neilson's outrage is that of the entrenched, righteous adjudicator with a goading aesthetic conscience; the hard heart who acts in the world through its furious condemnation. Tough on crime, Neilson sets up his review as a show trial, as if faced with the same dilemma as prosecutors of a known war criminal: "it is difficult to pick just one offence." The crimes of "repeat offender" Roy Miki are against puritanical normative standards of "style and taste," which the tropes of legality amplify to a universal register. Conscience rails because the example made by "irrelevant" corrupt institutions rewarding this "anti-poetry [that] deserved no award" (i.e., the antagonist of real poetry) threatens to spread the contagion. Roy Miki himself would furthermore underline the racialized dimension of Neilson's attack. When racially marked writing falls outside a given post-colonial economy of racial-ideological signs, it is unrecognisable as either racialised or as literature. Miki's book is expelled altogether from the definition of poetry. To Neilson, the book is both characterless and infuriating.

In order to complete the book, the reader must abandon the fruitless process of asking questions – a faculty necessary to enjoy poetry fully – and simply accept that this bland book isn't meant to make you feel or know anything. ("*Surrender*")

Neilson's comment about questions here deserves notice, being a shorthand form of exactly what many postmodern poets assert in their own poetics. Inquiry, question asking, critique, are poetry's imperatives. The difference is contextual and ideological. What Neilson means by asking questions is not what Nicole Brossard means by asking questions. They do not, would not, ask anything like the same questions, nor the same types of questions. Neilson's reasoning is bound in a very refined version of the dominant ideolect of the Canadian poetry reviewer, constrained by its narrow categories. So rather than ask new types of questions, as a confrontation with an unfamiliar poetic should prompt (as it did for Al Purdy), Neilson firmly applies the yardstick categories of the ideolect to an intransigent poetry. When those categories, those questions, predictably bend and break, he frames the failure as Miki's failure.

Postmodern, Ideology, Aesthetic Conscience

Radically Particular

If critical theory is to function as a subversive practice of decoding, un-doing and counter-coding dominant representational social codes, it must strive to operate as a revolutionary critique, in Henri Lefebvre's sense of "dialectical critique: understanding by transcending" (75). Lefebvre continues:

For bourgeois culture, like every ideology, has real content; it expresses and reflects something of the truth. The mystification lies in the presentation, use and fragmentation of that content; culture, taken as a whole, lives parasitically on this real content, which it has ceased to renew.... Revolutionary critique must expose this real content. (ibid.)

To perform critique in Lefebvre's sense, thought about poetry can never bind itself into the linguistic "restricted economy" (McCaffery, "Writing" 202) of normative evaluative criticism, "the fixed terminologies of bureaucratic and epistemological power" (Perelman, "Write" 168). Critical thinkers in poetics must never become mere technocrats of a jargon or ideolect. The analytical potential of terms like postmodern, ideology and conscience therefore lies in their dynamic instabilities which thwart instrumentality. A multiplicity of uses make the conceptual span of these terms so wide that they only acquire functional meaning in concrete impletion. Such dynamism is particularly characteristic of poetry, which as Bob Perelman writes, has available to it only "radically particular words" (ibid.). With such terms as postmodern, ideology and conscience "What

is more significant than the absence of a stable or singular definition ...
is that each definitional claim knowingly stakes itself against its com-
petitors" (Stacey, "Introduction" xiv). In this combative terminological
poiesis begins the longed-for "abolition of the boundary line between
poetry and theory" (Perelman, "Poetry" 166), a process which begins in
the terrain of theory and moves towards poetry. As Perelman celebrates
of Charles Bernstein's terminologically non-committal poetics: "[In *A
Poetics*] potential sites of definition become loci for counter-demon-
strations of a writing practice that disrupts any form of containment"
("Write" 312). Poetry, which "must remain undefined," can best oper-
ate as revolutionary critique in conditions of an open, general linguistic
economy. Perelman continues, in "Poetry In Theory:"

*Ultimately, it's all for the glory of poetry, which will remain ornamental
to the degree that it avoids the issues of power, history, bureaucracy, and
class that theory addresses. But theory also is in need of the particularity
and the sonic and rhetorical resources of poetry if its powerful but jargon-
heavy insights are to travel effectively outside the circuits of conferences
and graduate seminars.* (159)

Why Postmodern?

As Fredric Jameson writes, the case for the existence of a postmodernity "depends on the hypothesis of some radical break or *coupure*, generally traced back to the end of the 1950s or the early 1960s" ("Postmodernism" 1). Although evident continuities between the modern and postmodern lead me to think of the change as a *shift* or a *turn* rather than a *break*, Jameson's chronology seems acceptable. The 1950s are therefore a decade of postmodern genesis in poetry; the 1960s a decade of diaspora and popularisation; the 1970s the decade when postmodern poetry begins to exert its own limited hegemony, as some of its proponents and practitioners gain recognition and influence. By the mid-1970s the term "postmodern" (or "postmodernism") has become part of the dominant reviewer's ideolect, as a (usually derogatory) style tag.

Yet postmodernism is not a style. Postmodern poetry is not a unitary practice available for reviewers to point at. Anyone wishes to characterize new North American poetry since the 1960s faces a knotty dilemma. What term is both general enough to indicate the formally, aesthetically, and politically diverse set of poetic practices that arise after the modern passes the "post-," and is yet not a dilated catch-all for everything written in that historical period? And what term can mark changes in poetic practice as aspects of broader, extra-literary historical processes? Options exist.

Poetry critics still commonly use "avant-garde," an incendiary term entrenched in its modernist point of origin and in a rejected notion of progressive literary history. The term avant-garde embeds an obsolete

59

military metaphor of antagonistic, quasi-oedipal cultural struggle. Indeed, Pierre Bourdieu's model of the dynamics of the avant-garde fails in several respects to account for modes of sociality that emerge with postmodern writing communities. "Poetry ... lives in the hectic rhythm of the aesthetic revolutions which divide the continuum into extremely brief literary *generations*" (*Field* 52 emphasis in original). Rather, as Gregory Betts writes: "[P]ostmodern Canadian writers, in fact, used their writing to argue and demonstrate their belief that there was no 'behind' time to be ahead of." (153)

Ron Silliman's term *post-avant* situates recent poetry in a post-avant-garde phase. His term might therefore be better, except that in Silliman's model the post-avant begins in the 1980s, apparently so that Silliman can retain the heroic connotations of avant-garde as a rank stripe for the L = A = N = G = U = A = G = E poets of his own generation.[3] Charles Bernstein's *inventive poetry* improves on, without entirely avoiding, the teleology of techno-aesthetic progress implied in another recurrent term, *innovative*. Both terms, however, figure the poet as a harmless eccentric tinkerer, perhaps de-engineering what tanka poet Ishikawa Takuboku called "sad toys" for a depressed literary economy.

Scientistic and trivializing, *experimental* is worst. Experimental implies that the texts are laboratory reports from an "aesthetic realm unaffected by social determinants" (Derksen 57). It skirts the fact that in much of the poetry of the 20th century and after, the very openness of a text, its unfinished, speculative character, is actively reinscribed as a positive value. It thereby demonstrates an insensate misapprehension of divergent aesthetic imperatives, a misapprehension evidenced in the recurrent mistaken assumption that poets try (and fail) to obtain the old

---

3 David Lehman, in his book *The Last Avant-Garde* (1998), makes a rival parallel claim for the "New York School" poets Frank O'Hara, John Ashbery, James Schuyler and Kenneth Koch.

effects by new means. Here, new poetries are wrong-headed attempts to superficially retool old-garde poetic values into weird new-garde shapes. New poetries can only licitly be as Clint Burnham described bpNichol's *Martyrology*: "a liberal humanism expressed in postmodern praxis" (26). The final point here is the crux: Postmodernism is not a style. As Jameson writes, it is: "essential to grasp postmodernism not as a style but as a cultural dominant: a conception which allows for the presence and the coexistence of a range of very different, yet subordinate, features" ("Postmodernism" 4).

Finally – but not exhaustively – Pauline Butling calls attention in her essay "Re: Reading the Postmodern: Mess is Lore" to three other proposed terms: *radical* (Butling and Susan Rudy); *poetics of inquiry* (Christine Stewart); *engaged poetics* (Jeff Derksen) (334). The problem with each of these is that they imply that a Leftist, liberatory, or revolutionary critique inhere in the form or content (rather than address, intent, imperative or effect) of the writings. None of these three are general enough to capture the divergent political trajectories of new poetries. Nor can self-annointed *engaged* or *radical* poets, as committed to justice as they might be, afford any complacency about the political meanings of their works. As Michèle Barrett writes:

Meaning is not immanent; it is constructed in the consumption of the work. Hence, no text can be inherently progressive or reactionary; it becomes so in the act of consumption. There may be an authorial 'preferred reading' but the effects may be different from, even opposite to, those intended. Whatever the formal properties of a work, its ideological content, its 'political' implications, are not given. They depend on the construction that takes place at the level of consumption. (702)

With the term *postmodern*, chosen against the alternatives above, I hope to re-raise the spectre of a profound historical change that irrevocably alters how poetry is conceived and practiced. Further, the term's hybridity indicates that the postmodern is an extension of the modern – one that incorporates the modern without surpassing or escaping it. As Henri Lefebvre writes: "Modernity as ideology may be coming to an end, but modernism as technological practice goes from strength to strength" (94). The postmodern is another phase of development along the trajectory of the modern, if not another phase in the cultural (after) life-cycle of the modern. (Critics such as Alex Callinicos, in *Against Postmodernism: A Marxist Critique* accurately note that the stylistics and poetics supposedly specific to the postmodern are directly prefigured in certain strains of modernist literature.) Robert Stacey extends this argument, writing that:

[I]n other words, postmodernism was modernism's *unavoidably frustrated attempt to name its own future, or to name the cultural space of its own 'outside'.... [W]e might choose to read the disappearance of the postmodern, but, on the contrary, as the end of* modernism ... *and as the true beginning of a postmodernism finally empowered to name itself.* ("Introduction: Post-" xxiv)

In this line, Gregory Betts quotes another passage from Lyotard, who challenges the notion of the "post" as a mile-marker of progressive history: "A work can become modern only if it is first postmodern. Postmodernism thus understood is not modernism at its end but in the nascent state, and this state is constant" (161-2). Against the constructions of the postmodern in past tense, the period I mark with the term postmodernity remains unfinished.

A phase unfinished, or in the terms of art critic Hal Foster, ongoing in a "condition of aftermath," or a quasi undead "living on." The spectre of fearsome transformation Jameson raised was, as Foster points out, like Adorno's: the postmodern seems to bode "the end of art" (124) because it directly challenges, attacks, or circumvents so many value categories formerly fundamental to the definition of art. In "This Funeral is for the Wrong Corpse," Foster returns to Adorno to reposition an argument about the history of philosophy. He writes

Adorno ['s] riddle about the relevance of philosophy opens his Negative Dialectics *(1966): 'Philosophy, which once seemed absolute, lives on because the moment to realize it was missed.' ... [W]onder if this parallel guided Adorno [in his analysis of modernist art], and, further, if we might substitute 'art' where he writes 'philosophy'. In this case, might art be granted the ambiguous stay of sentence that Adorno grants philosophy – the possibility of 'living on'?* (123)

Self-consciously writing of the postmodern now, I necessarily write entirely in "the condition of aftermath," (126), when the term postmodern seems attenuated. It can be no other way. No term will be satisfactory. Ours is a (lengthening) moment of neo-neo, post-post, trans-trans, when art's own sanctioned narratives undermine the clarity of art and poetry's relationship to historical conditions.

Therefore, I resuscitate the vexed or dead term postmodern:

1 Because the formula post + modern, functioning as a temporal marker, indicates an historical shift that is not a liquidation of the modern period, but a shift that incorporates that period. Foster characterizes early articulations of the postmodern:

Implicit in this account is that postmodernist art was initially 'propped' on modernist categories, with all the ambiguity of (in) dependence implied by the word, but that it soon 'troped' these categories, in the sense that it treated them as so many completed practices or given terms to be manipulated as such. ("Funeral" 127)

2 Because postmodern suggests a change more comprehensive than (surface) stylistic or (surface) aesthetic. It connotes a paradigm shift

– a profound change in modes of production that affects culture on every level, rather than a shift into an ahistorical "paradigm-of-no-paradigm" (Foster 128). Jameson wrote of postmodernity as a question of "mutations in thinking or consciousness." Such mutations did take place, and from the early 1960s onwards, deeply recondition the poetic field.

3 Because the alternatives above, and others not discussed here, have an insidious, confounding metaphoricity. Postmodern, emerging from a tropological account of history, is a compound abstraction, preferable to more charismatic metaphor-laden alternatives because it therefore remains more open to radically particular concrete impletion.

4 Because it is inexact enough to allow for the internal coexistence of contradictory tendencies. As Hal Foster aerates the concept, the postmodern is far more than the schizophrenic condition Jameson describes, far more than a play of surfaces across surfaces. Only a speculative, still-contested polyvalent term like postmodern can even gesture towards the irreducible plurality (in terms of divergent political affiliations, formal strategies, reading practices, etc.) of new poetries emergent in Canada since the early 1960s.

5 Because the temporality implied by the term is open-ended. It does not suggest a bounded period, but "the time after...." However, it does suggest historical contingency, and thus resituates discussions of poetry since the 1960s in a broadly historical context. Critically, the history of the term postmodern originates in a critique of capital. The term postmodern registers changes in capitalist modes of production. Unlike several of the alternate terms, it does not redact capitalism from the historical picture, nor decouple this poetry from its embeddedness in capitalist culture. I take up the term, therefore, to combat posthistorical and postpolitical neo-culturisms that obfuscate historicity.

6 For lack of a better term. As Hal Foster again writes:

[although] the recursive strategy of the 'neo' appears as attenuated today as the oppositional logic of the 'post' is tired: neither suffices as a strong

64

paradigm for artistic or critical practice, and no other model stands in their stead. ("Funeral" 128)

In characterizing (once again) this whole unfinished phase as postmodern, I extend Foster's speculation: "Maybe this living-on is not a repeating so much as a making-new or simply a making-do with what-comes-after, a beginning again and/or elsewhere" (129).

Ideology Dog Breathalyzer

If, as Terry Eagleton complains, there are "almost as many theories of ideology as there are theorists of it" ("Introduction" 14), this variability is a good reason for a poetics to adopt the term. I root my concept of ideology in a certain trajectory of ideology critique that extends from Louis Althusser's foundational essay "Ideology and Ideological State Apparatuses," into current research in developmental psychology, sociolinguistics and cognitive linguistics. To begin with, Althusser writes:

[I]deology is not an aberration or a contingent excrescence of history: it is a structure essential to the historical life of societies. Further, only the existence and the recognition of its necessity enable us to act on ideology and transform ideology into an instrument of deliberate action on history.... Human societies secrete ideology as the very element and atmosphere indispensable to their historical respiration and life. (88)

Yet ideology remains a term commonly used as a pejorative, to indicate the false consciousness condition of an opponent or antagonist. In this familiar misuse, Eagleton writes, "ideology, like halitosis, is … what the other person has" (*Ideology* 2). I engage a concept of ideology that admits little such pejorative inflection, because its point of departure is not a false consciousness model of truth versus illusion. In developmental psychology, researchers often use the term "schema" where a Marxist thinker would use ideology (i.e., culturally specific beliefs, individually inflected). Ideology is the basic cognitive, linguistic and affective operating system of any socialized subject. To psychologists, schemas are

consistent core beliefs and patterns of thinking ... underlying cognitive
structures [that] form the basis for individuals' specific perceptions ...
blueprints or master plans that construct, organize, and transform peoples'
interpretations and predictions. (Lochman 312)

Although ideological tropes are often deliberately applied in poetry
book reviews, it is the unconscious character of ideology that matters
most, because it directs thought without active consent. Ideology, then,
is more a question of a spontaneous commonsense, and of a political
unconscious, than of reasoned assent to specific propositional contents.
As Althusser explains in "Marxism and Humanism:"

In truth, ideology has very little to do with 'consciousness', even supposing
this term to have an unambiguous meaning. It is profoundly unconscious,
even when it presents itself in a reflected form (as in pre-Marxist 'philoso-
phy'). Ideology is indeed a system of representations, but in the majority of
cases these representations have nothing to do with 'consciousness': they are
usually images and occasionally concepts, but it is above all as structures
that they impose on the vast majority of men, not via their 'consciousness.'
(233)

In Althusser's sense, ideology, then, is embodied materially in human
social practices. Language is among the core media that materialise and
embody ideology. As Pascal wrote: "Kneel down and move your lips in
prayer, and you will believe" (qtd. in Althusser, "Ideology" 168). Lan-
guage use is as material, as embodied, as bare knees on a cold cathedral
floor.

The specifically linguistic aspect of materialized ideology is charac-
terised by Slavoj Žižek in the preface to *Welcome to the Desert of the Real!*
He discovers a useful explanatory analogy in a joke about "The Missing
Ink." The joke, in full:

In an old joke from the defunct German Democratic Republic, a German worker gets a job in Siberia; he is aware of how all mail will be read by censors, he tells his friends: 'Let's establish a code: if a letter you get from me is written in ordinary blue ink, it's true; if it's written in red ink, it's false.' After a month, his friends get the first letter, written in blue ink: 'Everything is wonderful here: the shops are full, food is abundant, apartments are large and properly heated, cinemas show films from the West, there are many beautiful girls ready for an affair – the only thing you can't get is red ink.' (2)

As Žižek explicates this, our ideological condition under the more "refined conditions of liberal censorship" is similarly the matter of lacking means to describe our condition. He writes:

One starts by agreeing that one has all the freedoms one wants – then one merely adds that the only thing missing is 'red ink': we 'feel free' because we lack the very language to articulate our unfreedom. (2)

Everyday examples of the linguistic-ideological lack of ink, as Žižek would have it, abound. On the night of the 2006 Canadian federal election, for example, the election results were reported on CBC television thus: "Conservatives: 124 // Liberals: 103 // Bloc: 51 // NDP: 29 // Other: 1" (Mancini "Journal"). The question to ask of ideology is: who is the Other 1? White suprematism? Ozone restoration? Militant Veganism? Yogic levitation? Earth First!? Four inadequate terms compress a whole spectrum. Furthermore, whatever shreds of alterity *do* remain in Canadian parliamentary politics are completely disarticulate. The content of alterity is unsayable. The use of the convenient positional term "Other" in that CBC report has strong ideological implications.

As this pertains to poetry book reviews in Canada, the situation is slightly different than in Žižek's example – it is more akin to the CBC example. The *ink* is overlooked, rather than strictly absent. Unlike the Siberia of Žižek's joke, the appropriate inks, so rarely used, are available for poetry reviewers in the Great White North. The situation entices me to imagine the scene at the reviewer's desk. Picture several pots of ink laid out – blue, red, green, purple, black, yellow. Say the blue ink is the ink of the dominant review ideolect, and each of the others is an alternative that might be commensurate to the aesthetic imperatives of a target poet. In this scene, when the discursive ritual begins, although all the right inks might be available, the reviewer passes them over. What remains to investigate is why they are passed over. Is there a cultural taboo (i.e., "I see them there – but one just doesn't use those inks for writing book reviews")? Do reviewers programmatically refuse to use other colours (i.e., as Bruce Serafin might say: "I will not write reviews in that academic-corporate-communist-anti-individualist ink!")? Does ideology make the other inks invisible during the review-writing ritual?

Žižek's startlingly apt analogy can be misleading, however, if one takes its focus on the missing ink as exhaustive of the problem. The practice of writing reviews in the inherited dominant terms (blue ink) causes reviewers to try to shoehorn profoundly different poetics in to a narrow set of categories. In a space of possibles with an enormous number of positions for poets to occupy, a severely limited ideolect crushes the variety of positions into a handful of stylistic categories. In the ideolect of the CBC's report on the federal election, for example, mainstream political alterity is merely a structural position, with no substantive content except its otherness. Similarly, to many poetry reviewers, writing impertinent to dominant categories is often (merely and entirely) non-poetry or anti-poetry.

The failure of poetry reviewing practices to pluralize along with their putative object, poetry, is an illustration drawn in missing ink. This side of the linguistic-ideological question is what Andrew Goatly addresses in his book *Washing the Brain: Ideology and Hidden Metaphor*. Drawing directly from the work of George Lakoff, Goatly articulates a distinction between live versus dead metaphors, a distinction that can expand to include live versus dead tropes and concepts. Goatly writes:

If we call conventional metaphors "dead" or "inactive," this is because they are old and their interpretation does not demand as much conscious activity on our part. But this does not mean to say that they have less effect on our cognition. In fact, it is precisely because they are conventionalized that they may achieve the power to subconsciously affect our thinking, without our being aware of it. (22)

In poetry reviewing, the tropes or metaphors, ritually elaborated in aesthetic reasoning, determine the forms value judgements will take – the unconscious character of ideology. Imagine for a moment two rival reviews of the same poet that differently characterize the same features: 1) Nelson Ball's minimalist poems erupt like breaths of wind in long dry grass; subtle, resonant, fleeting. 2) Nelson Ball's microscopic poem-trinkets are, at best, a poetic idler's chew-toys. A few pages later in his study, Goatly takes a stronger position:

The scale of metaphorical effect runs in the opposite direction from the scale of ideological effect, precisely because with literal language and conventional metaphors the ideology is latent, and therefore all the more powerful. (Washing 29)

Through Aesthetic Conscience

In his loosely narrative poem, "I Journeyed Through Russia," poet Yevgeny Yevtushenko uses the conceit of a nostalgic automobile journey (in a Soviet-produced car called a Moskvich) to the shrine of Leo Tolstoy to depict the transformative enlightenment and development of a Soviet-specific aesthetic conscience. The poem opens on a scene of Yevtushenko (the poem's narrator) doubled over in severe night-pangs of bad conscience, symptom of what appears to be an early-onset (or preemptive) midlife crisis:

> *I am past thirty. I fear the nights.*
> *I hunch the sheet with my knees.*
> *I bury my face in the pillow, shamefully weeping,*
> *that I have squandered my life on little nothings*
> *and in the morning will squander it again.*
>
> *If only you had known, my critics*
> *whose goodness is so innocently under question,*
> *how tender thundering condemnation seems*
> *compared with my own scolding,*
> *you would be relieved, if late at night*
> *you found your conscience tormenting you unjustly.*
> *When leafing through all my verse*
> *I find this: by squandering myself so rashly*
> *I have soiled the ages with so much rot. (480)*

Through the 280+ lines that follow, in a mixture of speculative digression and narration, Yevtushenko details the formation of aesthetic conscience in all its dynamic facets. I draw Yevtushenko's poem into this discussion not to endorse its Leninism or nationalism, but to demonstrate the robust homology of conscience and aesthetic conscience in a cultural context very different from that of the Canadian poetic field. Conscience is an apparatus of ideology crucial to the formation of subjecthood. Althusser holds, like Nietzsche and Hegel, that there can be no human subject socialized under capitalism who does not have conscience. (Some of the convergences between Althusser, Nietzsche and Hegel on questions of conscience are examined below.) As an apparatus of ideology, conscience is equally historical, subject-specific and site-specific, and contingent on standpoint. Rather than being unitary, conscience is subject to a pluralization in concrete social grammars; the same person may harbour several incompatible consciences. Aesthetic conscience, as part of the broader territory of conscience, must be considered from the same perspective.

Note that the term "aesthetic conscience" is not my coinage; it is used in rival, contradictory ways from at least the mid-19th century onwards. Most often the term is invoked obliquely, cast as a shadow of other debates. An early occurrence of the term in English is found in a 1853 article by Robert Hogarth Patterson entitled "Real and Ideal Beauty," republished in his 1862 book *Essays in History and Art*. In subsequent decades, the term appears more frequently, well past the mid-20th century, until the term "aesthetic" itself loses currency in critical discourse. Aesthetic conscience is, instead, normally used as if the term's intelligibility can be assumed. This in itself is crucial evidence that aesthetic and moral conscience are, in most cases, already understood to be either parallel, homologous, equivalent – or wholly identical.

Again: conscience is a robust, mobile structure (a process, not a thing) made up of dynamic components. Conscience is core to the constitution of the socialised human subject and to the reproduction of ideology.

Conscience is a system of relationships between four major constitutive components: moral affect, moral identity/moral self, moral reasoning and moral competence. These, at the site of the concrete deed, of action, are thickly mediated by the person's perception of moral atmosphere. Conscience emerges fully in human subjects after a cohesion between identity and affect is ignited by the acquisition of a moral language – an *ideolect* – sufficient for moral reasoning. From that stage, the components of reason, identity and affect can be accorded in moral competence – which is to say that the dynamic components of conscience can work in concert towards conscionable outcomes.

Schiller describes the superlunary subject of conscience: the moral genius. The moral genius is variously named, with distinct evaluative inflections, as the "beautiful soul" (Goethe and Schiller), the "hard heart" (Hegel), or the "virtuoso" (Shaftesbury) or "Thomas Gradgrind" (Dickens). The Common Sense Police. In each case, excellent moral competence is the defining characteristic. As Schiller writes:

With a 'beautiful soul', therefore, it is not really the individual actions but rather the entire character which is moral.... Thus in a 'beautiful soul' sensibility and reason, duty and inclination, harmonize; such a soul is expressed phenomenally as grace. (qtd. in Gram 318)

The only sequential priority of conscience is in initial development; moral affect is present before moral reasoning begins. Once conscience emerges, however, no single component necessarily dominates, nor has sequential priority. The components interact (and affect each other) in unpredictable ways specific to each individual.

What is the relationship of aesthetic to moral conscience? Aesthetic conscience is the result of an annexation by morality of the realm of the sensory. Annexed by morality, the realm of the sensory becomes the judgmental mode of perception: it becomes aesthetics. A useful, general definition of the aesthetic could be: the territory of sensation annexed to the empire of value. As Terry Eagleton writes in "The Ideology of the Aesthetic," this annexation is socially imperative:

Structures of power must become structures of feeling and the name for this mediation from property to propriety is the aesthetic. If politics and aesthetics are deeply at one, it is because pleasurable conduct is the true index of successful social hegemony, self-delight the very mark of social submission. What matters in aesthetics is not art, but this whole project of reconstructing the human subject from the inside, informing its subtlest affections and bodily responses with this law which is not a law. (330)

Not that reviewers and critics, in particular, work to moralize aesthetics: Aesthetic discourse is always already moral discourse. In aesthetics, sensation is annexed to the empire of value. Aesthetic conscience is the administrative state apparatus, as it were, of morality's new colony.

The question is why this annexation occurs. If conscience is socially necessary, as Nietzsche argues in *On the Genealogy of Morality*, then what drives the exuberant hunger and territorial greed of morality that lead to aesthetics and the formation of aesthetic conscience? Eagleton, like Nietzsche, notes that morality is, at base, a struggle to tame impulses. Morality's main subjects and victims are the "rabble" of the senses (as Kant calls them). In Nietzsche's account of the formation of conscience, he points directly to this struggle; the socially necessary repression that leads directly to the historical emergence of conscience:

All instincts which are not discharged outwardly turn inwards – this is what I call the internalisation of man *[sic]: with it there now evolves in man what will later be called his 'soul'. The whole inner world, originally stretched thinly as though between two layers of skin, was expanded and extended itself and gained depth, breadth and height … man full of emptiness … had to create from within himself an adventure, a torture chamber,*

an unsafe and hazardous wilderness – this fool ... became the inventor of
'bad conscience.' (57)

The territorial expansion of conscience into aesthetics is compelled by art's direct, constant, unbroken tie to these ever-unruly realms of sense, desire, impulse and instinct. Art constantly re-stimulates those repressed impulses, those euphoric dimensions of experience that morality (through conscience, its administrative apparatus) must labour to put down. Thus the relationship of religious institutions with art has been historically unquiet. If the sensory lures of art provide a basis for mighty religious propaganda (intense sensation correctly value-managed), the passions stirred often exceed square piousness. Hence major social movements like Islamic iconoclasm; hence the Council of Trent in 1545 nearly bans music in the Catholic Church; hence protestants in the Southern US A burning piles of rock 'n' roll vinyl records.

Eagleton further ties the emergence of aesthetics (and so of aesthetic conscience) to the categorical splits produced by bourgeois social practice. "The aesthetic, as the moment of letting the world go and clinging instead to the formal act of knowing it, promises to re-unite those poles of subject and object, value and fact, reason and nature, which bourgeois social practice has riven apart" ("Ideology" 331). In these views, aesthetics can be seen either as a false promise to heal social contradictions or as liberatory or utopian in potential. The crucial point is that if every subject is always already the subject of conscience, as per Althusser, Nietzsche and Hegel, in North America and Western Europe today every active cultural consumer has aesthetic conscience.

Moral Surveillance

The argument of the identity of moral and aesthetic conscience is close to one made by Jacques-Bernard Roumanes, in a neo-Romantic polemic of 2000, "La conscience esthétique" [Aesthetic Conscience]. He regards aesthetic conscience as the pre-rational, pre-linguistic sensibility of childhood, and so locates aesthetic conscience not only as the actual origin of moral conscience, but of all intelligence and creativity. Roumanes posits:

l'art comme réalisation ultime de la science et de la morale, ou en termes plus contemporains, poser l'esthétique comme incarnation de la rationalité et de l'éthique, c'est montrer que la conscience esthétique coïncide, forme et force, avec l'expression du sentiment intérieur. (28)[4]

In this detail, the German hyper-Romantic poet Novalis prefigures Romanes' argument by two centuries in his novel *Heinrich van Oftedingen*. To Novalis, conscience is the source of all poetic creation.

I know only that phantasy is for me the entire instrument of my present world. Even conscience – this power that produces sense and the world,

---

4 "art as the ultimate realisation of science and of morality, or, in more contemporary terms, to posit the aesthetic as the incarnation of reason and morality is to show that aesthetic conscience coincides, in form and function, with the expression of internal feeling." [my translation]

this seed of all personality – appears to me as the spirit of the cosmic poem,
the accident of the eternal romantic coincidence of the infinitely changing
totality of life. (qtd. in Gram 320)

In this utopian line, based in an apparently selective reading of Rousseau,
Roumanes posits a return to a poetic, fundamentally innocent aesthetic
conscience, as the route to human salvation. Unlike Novalis' belief in the
coincidence of conscience with totality, Roumanes' unproblematic, un-
virulent, and overly responsive concept of conscience leads him to treat
artists as angelically childlike beings:

Tout le malheur de l'homme vient de ce qu'il est incapable de demeurer en
paix dans la chambre de sa vie. Sauf les enfants. Sauf les poètes. Sauf les
artistes. Sauf ceux dont la conscience esthétique demeure au fondement de
leur conscience cognitive. (29)[5]

Roumanes' and Novalis' core theme of conscience as fundamentally cre-
ative, erupts also in Nietzsche's *Genealogy*, where he finds in the ago-
nies of bad conscience the "true womb of ideal and imaginative events,
[which] brought a wealth of novel, disconcerting beauty and affirma-
tion to light, and perhaps for the first time, beauty *itself*" (59 emphasis
in original).

These concepts of conscience represent a secondary but important
stream in the discourse on the relationship of conscience and art. More
influential concepts emerge from the debate initiated in Hegel's critique
of Kant in his *Phenomenology of Spirit*. Michel Despland summarizes
Kant's notion of conscience, the one Hegel critiques, in his article "Can

---

5 "All the sorrows of man come from the fact that he is incapable of living in peace in
the chamber of his life. Except children. Except poets. Except artists. Except those
in whom aesthetic conscience sits at the foundation of their intellectual conscience."
[my translation]

Conscience Be Hypocritical?" Kantian morality is immanent, *out there* to be discovered. Its laws are ideal, transcendent, available, even if temporarily obscured. The only unimpeachable good in human society is good will. Art made from good motives, therefore, must be salutary. Kant treats morality, conscience (and life) mainly as a problem of knowledge. For the Kantian actor, the anxiety of conscience is in the desire to know if an action can be *judged* as moral or not, not in the consequences of action as such. To Kant, only an action taken out of duty, out of respect for moral law, can be a moral action. Intent and motive matter, whereas the concrete insertion of the deed into history is comparatively unimportant. Conscience's epistemological imperative is toward the universalization of its principles in maxims. So, for a deed to be moral it must be possible to draw from it a universal moral law. Its foundation in ideal morality and reason furthermore make conscience self-sufficient, and ultimately efficacious because: "A man cannot bribe his own reason" (qtd. in Despland 359). Writings in this Kantian, idealist line assume that conscience develops inexorably towards a unitary state, without contradiction. Robert Hogarth Patterson construes aesthetic conscience in this Kantian mode:

[Just] as the intellectual Conscience tells us what is True, and as the Moral one judges of Goodness or Virtue, so the aesthetic Conscience moulds, by the principles of beauty, the forms which through the medium of the Imagination are presented to the mental eye. To illustrate the process by a most simple case. Say there is presented to the eye a line on a black board stretching between two points, but not quite straight, – or a circle imperfectly drawn. Then forthwith the mind of the spectator says, "Not this line," or "not that circle;" and in their stead an ideal line or true circle is conceived by the mind, and is drawn in the mind's eye. (90)

Typical of 19th century uses of the term, Patterson connects aesthetic conscience directly, proudly, with Christian morality. One outcome of this strand of argument in review criticism is the equation of aesthetic with moral good. This is the site of most discussions of the moral and the aesthetic, summarized in the conventional question: "Can a work of art be morally evil yet at the same time aesthetically excellent?" Leavisite (and Kantian) aesthetics follow an imperative to affirm the ultimate social goodness of art, toward the same conclusions. If the work has morally dubious content but the critic still intuits its quality (i.e., believes/feels it is good), the answer often prescribed is: Excellent art has a morally salutary meaning in-and-of-itself, as an exemplar of human achievement. Where this adaptation can't be accomplished, aesthetic conscience drops the burdensome work from the canonic registry, or excludes it entirely from the definition of art – the relieved critic moves on, a few ounces lighter. To Patterson, as to Kant, the emergence of aesthetic conscience is flawlessly inductive: Ideal beauty trains conscience to know the beautiful and good. Aesthetic conscience is an effect of ideal form projecting its pattern through the misshapen actuality of concrete form. What arises when the process is complete must be simultaneously a moral and aesthetic good. To be licit, a work of art must be good in both senses.

Typical as Patterson's formulation is of its moment, and much like the terms ideology and postmodern, as the term aesthetic conscience passes through different contexts it becomes an ideologeme: it is subject to a higher degree of differential inflection and local impletion than all words already are. As an ideologeme, aesthetic conscience works friction-free in service of incompatible ideologies. Along a similar, although less metaphysical line than Patterson, one common conception of aesthetic conscience is as a reliable internal regulatory system, governed (disproportionately) by either aesthetic affect, aesthetic identity or aesthetic reasoning. Aesthetic conscience's main function, in these cases, is to divert the interpellated subject from aesthetically unconscionable decisions. Here, aesthetic conscience is often individual in expression, yet bound to transcendent formal principles that may be given or learned. Developmental psychology research into conscience begins with similar premises, making a distinction between "positive morality," which is the consensus morality of the group, and "personal morality," which is an individual's idiosyncratic, improvised morality. In the difference between these lies concrete social struggle. As Bert Musschenga writes "The divergences between personal moralities and positive moralit[ies] constitute the moral dynamics within a social group" (27). Note how well this accords with common constructions of poetic (or moral) genius; the greater the artist and artwork, the more efficacious his/her aesthetic conscience. In some cases, conscience is said to be precisely what lacks, where talent alone remains fuzzily indefinite. A self-assured Gustave Flaubert complains that: "Genius is not rare nowadays, but conscience is what nobody has and what one should strive after" (qtd. in Moore 8). Peter Bayne draws such a portrait of John Ruskin, genius of (affective) aesthetic conscience:

He [Ruskin] is so organised that an offence to beauty affects him as with a pang of literal pain, and it is equally certain that he never thinks of this pain as selfish, but attaches it to a moral quality, as if it were the sting of an aesthetic conscience – as if the duty were imposed upon him of protesting against the destruction of beauty as a sacrilege and a sin. (441-2)

Individualist formulations treat conscience as an individual process, not a collective one, sometimes in terms of a principled, lonely objection to an unacceptable state of affairs. Many reviewers of postmodern poetry, early in their careers in particular, anoint themselves with this righteous oil. Hegel aims one of his critiques specifically at such actors: "when anyone says that he is acting according to his own law and conscience against others, he is saying, in fact, that he is wronging them" (402). In moral discourse, Hegel terms this type of social actor the "Hard Heart," summarised by Moltke S. Gram as "the particular agent purporting to represent the moral order while condemning the universal evil of the age. The Hard Heart ... maintains a position in opposition to the prevailing moral climate of its time" (327). In these constructions, aesthetic conscience is an irresistible force that compels extraordinary individuals to make the risky decision to stand up against "the herd," against "mediocrity" or "the prevailing moral climate" or "status quo" or "those hypocrites" – or whatever term is used to signify a general, morally inferior antagonist. Henry van de Velde asks the principled question of the aesthetic Hard Heart: "Will no one stand up to assert the consciousness of having aesthetic conscience of his own and bring some spontaneous echo of his inner being, some genuinely individual contribution, to the furnishing of his own home?" (123).

A different, even genuinely antagonistic, ideology produces other dictates of aesthetic conscience, while the formal structure persists. In particularly vanguardist variations, the problematic that the Hard Heart faces is made social. "Innovative" artistic strategies, such as the diverse compositional strategies in postmodern poetics, are constructed as specific sites of discursive resistance to unconscionable social conditions. New poetry enacts new formal strategies as interventions into actual hegemony. Modern and postmodern literatures moralize aesthetics in this Gramscian vein: The aesthetic conscience of the vanguard won't let them be satisfied with half measures, with inherited forms, nor with conditions as they are. The duty of a vanguard worth the badge is to pursue the logic of a social-aesthetic proposition right to its explosive end. Such is Jacques Barzun's picture of mid-19th century vanguards, with aesthetic consciences powered by bitter disgust and disaffection:

With the onset of industrialization, the uglification of cities, the visible degradation of the masses, the demagogy and sensationalism of the penny press, the cheapening of taste through the early crude mass production, the raucousness of advertising, the emotional disturbances connected with the change from manual to mechanical work that makes a cipher – with all these and a dozen other consequences of man's entry into the industrial age, the moral and aesthetic conscience of the West, manifesting itself through its artists, began to repudiate society as a whole. (175)

84

To art critic Clive Bell, aesthetic conscience is oriented in a similar, oppositional direction, towards transformative change in art practice, rather than towards protective normativity or repression of illicit impulses. Rather than a pious Catholic conscience, he names an impulsively revolutionary aesthetic conscience. Bell constructs aesthetic conscience as a force that provokes artists to confront and subvert commonsense assumptions, through a determined reading of the formal and stylistic dimensions of art in political-moral terms. Note his presumed parallel of moral with aesthetic conscience, and the identitarian inflection:

As the twentieth century dawns, a question, which up to the time of the French Revolution had been judiciously kept academic, shoulders its way into politics: 'Why is this good?' About the same time, thanks chiefly to the Aesthetes and the French Impressionists, an aesthetic conscience, dormant since before the days of the Renaissance, wakes and begins to cry, 'Is this art?' (qtd. in Reed 191)

Octavio Paz's concept of aesthetic conscience has a similar moral stance, with aesthetic reasoning as the governing component of the process. Paz credits Charles Baudelaire with giving the group affects and identities of 20th century art movements the means with which to speak. Without such means, without an ideolect, there is no conscience. Paz writes: "Baudelaire's thought gave a critical and aesthetic conscience to almost all the artistic movements of our time, from impressionism to the present" (60). Paz's is an example of a the quasi-mystical figuration of the dead Master as overseer of conscience; both as eyes, ears, and voice of conscience, and as the phantasm to whom conscience is answerable. Baudelaire becomes a watchman over modernists everywhere. As Nietzsche wrote: "the ancestor himself is transfigured into a god." (61)

In the second chapter of *On the Genealogy of Morality*, Nietzsche takes up the question of conscience in greater depth. Although the main accent is on the concept of conscience as a repressive apparatus originating in the memory of punishment – essentially the concept engaged by researchers in developmental psychology – when Nietzsche uses the term outside his attempts at its definition, conscience appears contradictory, dynamic, variable and site-specific. Nietzsche deploys portmanteaus like "scientific conscience," "bad conscience," "Christian conscience" without explication, and overtly separates the conscience of the "nobler clans," or the conscience of the "dominant instinct" from others consciences. For Nietzsche, conscience has no single, guaranteed moral content, not even within the same human subject. Two moralities can appear "in harsh juxtaposition … in the same person" (*Daybreak* 154). In light of this internal contestation, Nietzsche's use of the specific term "aesthetic conscience" in *Human, All Too Human* suggests that conscience has a straightforwardly normative function. Provided no Nietzschean snare is set in the term "fanaticism," the Great Historicizer, journeyer beyond good and evil, the proto-deconstructionist poet-philosopher, diagnoses artistic vanguards as having pathologically underdeveloped aesthetic affect. Parallel to positivist developmental psychology, anti-social or wicked behaviour evinces moral incompetence, which is to say it evinces a lack of conscience. Without moral competence, conscience does not form. In this form, Nietzsche's is a type of judgement often made by reviewers hostile to postmodern poetry:

Those with no aesthetic conscience. – *The actual fanatics of an artistic faction are those completely inartistic natures who have not penetrated even the elements of artistic theory or practice but are moved in the strongest way by all the elemental effects of an art. For them there is no such thing as aesthetic conscience – and therefore nothing to hold them back from fanaticism.* (133)

Conscience as the Administrative Apparatus of Ideology

A 2010 collection of developmental psychology research papers entitled *The Development and Structure of Conscience* (TDASOC), edited by Willem Koops, Daniel Brugman, Tamara J. Ferguson and Andries F. Sanders[6], provides a practical structural model for conceptualizing the

---

6 Although my purpose here is not to launch a critique of developmental psychology, if I am to use concepts drawn from this collection effectively – and in good conscience – it is necessary to articulate some of my critiques of the assumptions it is founded upon and the projects it represents. Specifically, the researchers in TDASOC too often work from classist concepts of a fixed, noncontingent, even Kantian, morality. Almost all start in the untenable position that conscience is a unified (although complex), efficacious social regulator of good behaviour. No clear or sustained discrimination is made between Christian-residual moral code and historically arbitrary state law. One result is that historically site-specific behaviours are flattened into a plane of the "immoral." Petty crime (such as marijuana use), is treated with the same analytical tools as acts of violence. Yet if the research is initiated in a Kantian vein, data often brings researchers marginally closer to a Hegelian critique as they are confronted with conscience's adaptive, self-serving, subjectivist, structurally hypocritical character. As Tjeert Olthof notes "moral judgements [by which he means moral reasoning, as tested via an administered questionnaire] predicted the subjects' moral hypocrisy rather than their actual morally relevant behaviour" (333). Olthof concludes that "the same level of moral reasoning can be used to justify contradictory moral judgements" (329), yet the scientific practice is not transformed by such discoveries, made again and again throughout the book. As Hegel argues, conscience's structural imperative is often only towards self-consistency and

87

processes of conscience versus aesthetic conscience. Given my heavy disclaimers in the footnote below, and granted that much remains to critique in their methodologies, a project of conscience critique can productively appropriate both the core structural concepts and researchers' specific observations about development and behaviour. Further, in spite of the methodological problems, their very scientism helps conceive of a socially constituted conscience, without idealist or metaphysical content.

TDASOC figures conscience, (i.e., the administrative apparatus) of ideology, as an aggregate of several overlapping components. Con-

---

universalization of principles of its own convictions; so Olthof discovers that "children who do bully do not necessarily soften their moral judgements about bullying in order to keep those judgements consistent with their own behaviour" (334). Although she goes on to make remarks connecting bullying behaviour in adolescents to "leadership qualities" (337), even noting known statistical correlations, the crucial next step of seeing that these adolescents in the cultural climate of neoliberalism can happily bully "in good conscience" – or even out of an emergent sense of capitalist principle! – is spectacularly missed. Again and again, through the analysis of data, ideology is *discovered* but it is never *admitted*. What makes these errors especially dangerous is what Hegel identified as the danger of the sincere moral actor. On the developmental path from everyday hypocrite to sincere moral actor, forms of evil arise. Michel Depland summarizes:

> While the hypocrite begins fully conscious of what he does, he can become trapped in his lies and sincerely believe – without a crack in his sincerity – that he is in fact what he claims to be ... an attitude that once was put on as a front can progressively, even insensibly, become a sincere conviction ... in time 'conscience' [is] flattered ... with its exalted authority ... the so called sincere moral man becomes worse than the hypocrite (367).

The point here is the one that it is most important to make about hate crimes, for example, that they are better understood not as crimes of passion, but as crimes of principle. Hatred often acts in good, healthy, self-certain conscience. Perhaps an eventual sequel to *TDASOC* will show a research practice transformed, but as it stands the work here is based in far too many indefensible assumptions.

science is not a thing, it is a process, and an indispensable apparatus of ideology based on a dynamic system of relationships between several structuring components. Although conscience forms a coherent (but porous and supple) whole, the strength of any one of its components is insufficient to describe how efficaciously conscience functions, nor why it really functions at all. Again, the components are:

· moral affect
· moral identity/moral self
· moral reasoning
· moral competence

As Willem Koops *et al.* write, *discovering* but not *admitting* the presence of ideology, each "component involves a complex set of processes that can operate differentially in individuals as a function of cultural, historical, developmental and social influences" (2). Furthermore, "perception of moral atmosphere" (13) – which emerges from the interaction of these components – densely mediates moral behaviour. Moral atmosphere is what seems permissible in a specific social situation, the trained sense that what is allowable in one social situation may not be allowable in another. Conscience works as it does because it is an empty structure. It has no universal nor inherent content, only the specific content given to it by an ideology. One of Hegel's most radical critiques of Kantian conscience is here. "Conscience ... in the majesty of its elevation above specific law and every content of duty, puts whatever content it pleases into its willing and knowing" (397). Conscience can serve any moral order. This emptiness is also the quality that makes it so susceptible to mediation through perception of moral atmosphere. Hence the true cliché of the Toronto peace officer who beats a pacifist protester half to death in Queen's Park, then goes home to be a loving father. Or that of the compassionate Socialist presidential candidate who also rapes hotel maids. These men, who "know right and wrong," do not need to have troubled consciences. The combination of these factors – conscience's emptiness and its mediation – help account for its day-to-day efficacy, how it curbs certain extreme behaviours. Yet in the moral atmosphere of war, in contrast, much that would be unconscionable in civilian life is imperative of military duty.

As to the interaction of components, once operant, conscience is a system of feedback in which any of the components can affect, and transform, any of the others. A subject can reason him/herself towards new feelings; new feelings can initiate new reflections (see Koops *et al.* 12), new identity concepts can introduce or be the result of new affect – in any combination imaginable. Among the many characteristics of conscience is its adaptability, again predicated on its structural robustness and essential emptiness. Aesthetic conscience, finally, is only an extension of the territory of conscience into the contested realm of the senses, an annexation of the realm of sensation to the realm of value.

Moral Affect

Moral affect is the system of moral feelings, the system of feelings related to moral evaluations. It is a set of affective representations of the rules of conduct. The presence of moral feelings – such as guilt, shame, anticipatory anxiety, righteousness, certain modes of pride or empathy – demonstrate that moral rules have become part of the subject's bodily life. Moral affect is initially adequate to produce desired/acceptable moral behaviour – a subject can know what he/she *should* do from early on, before conscience fully emerges. Koops, Brugman and Ferguson agree that "rationalization (a defensive strategy) is neither usual nor necessary" (8). On the basis of moral affect alone, subjects can make the "right" moral choices, those appropriate to the moral atmosphere, or may sense when a behaviour is "wrong" without being able to reason out why. To bridge Althusser with developmental psychology, this is to suggest that "the law" is internalized to the point that it becomes a source of pre-linguistic or extra-linguistic affect, or embodied nervous response. Similarly, a poet can spontaneously produce work perfectly appropriate for a given cultural context. (As Frank O'Hara wrote: "You just go on your nerve.") Olthof terms this a "'social intuitionist'" model of morality, which accords with Hegel: "According to the model, moral judgements are based on affective and other intuitive processes and moral reasoning only serves to justify" (329).

Comparatively, Hegel writes of the self-certain affective base of conscience, that its "intention, through being its own intention, is what is right; all that is required is that it should know this, and should state its conviction that its knowing and willing are right" (397). Yet, however fundamental moral affect is to conscience, affect is also a source and site of contradictions, friction, slippage. Terwogt *et al.* observe that "judgements and feelings do not always provide a similar picture … [because] moral feelings are often mixed with other, more basic, feelings that do not answer to the rules of cognition" (217). In line with Eagleton's view on aesthetics and sensation, and Nietzsche's concept of conscience as repression, I suggest that this is because of affect's link to feeling, and so to the creaturely life the body. Affect may or may not heed the interpellative hail of moral reason. As Max Raphael writes: "Art frees us from enslavement to words, concepts and false moral values by showing us that life knows differentiations that cannot be reduced to concepts as well as situations which cannot be judged by accepted moral standards" (qtd. in Barrett 705). Here, thinkers like Eagleton discover that aesthetic conscience is a hot zone within the wider territory of conscience, as the contact with art constantly re-stimulates base feelings, and incites dilemma.

Moral Identity/Moral Self

Keller *et al.* write that moral affect is a "central aspect of the moral self and [has] a double function: interpersonally to maintain or re-establish a 'moral balance' in social relationships; intra-individually to maintain or re-establish consistency with the moral self" (256). Moral identity, or moral self, is "a self-conception organised around a set of moral traits" (Olthof 334). Although moral affect may be sequentially primary, moral identity is just as core. Until a person becomes conscious of him/herself as a moral agent – a consciousness achieved through a combination of ideolect and affect – conscience does not form. As Hegel writes, the "*existent reality* of conscience … is one which is a *self*, an existence which is conscious of itself, the spiritual element of being recognised and acknowledged" (388). In aesthetic conscience in particular, identity is often a dominant component. Poets' and reviewers' aesthetic self-conceptions can be assertively articulate. The type of aesthetic subjects (consumers or producers) they construct themselves as have a determinant role on outcomes. That is to say, their aesthetic identities structure their practices as critics and poets. Such identities are both individual and affiliative, related to group affects of belonging (to a movement, a crowd, a type, a discourse, etc.), and to willed individuation – the efforts of reviewers or poets make to distinguish themselves, to be different, to stand out. The strength of such identities appears to be dependent on the degree of self-conscious integration of "beliefs and values" into the subject's "sense of self" (Olthof 334). If Schiller's 'beautiful soul' is mainly a competent agent, Hegel's Hard Heart primarily projects identity as will through

93

critical judgement: "The only action the Hard Heart undertakes is condemnation" (Gram 327).

Above all, in its role as a pillar of conscience, moral identity does not welcome the threats posed by dilemmas, whether internal or external. Conscience's virulent or adaptive moves of self-preservation are motivated by categorical challenges that threaten moral identity. Predominantly, conscience either reacts by adaptation or rejection. If a threat is external, the issue can be promptly resolved through the act of righteous condemnation: terminal judgement. The categories hold firm; the challenge is categorically rejected. Confronted with internal dilemmas (such as evidence of its own hypocrisy) rather than force the person to change behaviour conscience more often adapts its terms to re-define the behaviour. To protect its quietude – a dominant structural imperative of conscience – and to protect moral identity, conscience will shift its terms, change the meaning of its categories, so that the behaviour, by definition, is no longer hypocritical[7]. Aesthetic conscience, when aesthetic identity is threatened by novel new works, uses both means. Either it changes the definition of art to accommodate the work, or holds categories firm to exclude the work from the definition of art. Hegel writes that: "What conscience places before them ... they must dispose of it in their own consciousness, nullify it by judging and explaining it in order to preserve their own self" (395). This self-protective zeal arises partly from the fact that moral self/identity is the component of conscience which subjects most consciously, actively and passionately construct. (A far smaller number actively construct and elaborate the ideolect of moral reason, by comparison.) Through moral identity, people become active contributors to their own subjugation to the administrative apparatus of con-

---

7   The George W. Bush Presidential Administration famously demonstrated a
    collective moral competence of the latter kind. When confronted about their use
    of torture, a threat to collective US American moral identity, they changed the
    definition of torture to make their practices conscionable.

94

science, as they teach themselves, literally, to identify with the structure. In Althusser, as in Hegel above, and in Nietzshe, such identification is, in the last instance, necessary for subjecthood to emerge at all. As Judith Butler writes in "Conscience Doth Make Subjects of Us All": "a subject is formed through the passionate pursuit of the reprimanding recognition of the state" (24). This identification also seems to provide the subject a guarantee of existence otherwise withheld. Butler elaborates:

According to the logic of conscience, one in which Althusser appeared fully constrained, that passionate attachment to the law is that without which the linguistic guarantee of existence for the subject proves impossible. (25)

Threats to identity thus register in conscience, and in aesthetic conscience, as threats to existence.

Moral Reasoning

At this stage, one could ask: Does every art consumer have aesthetic conscience? While a conclusive answer to this question is unobtainable, I assume it would be near impossible to find any art consumer in Europe or North America right now who does not have aesthetic conscience. Everyone has enough exposure to cultural products to have at least developed a set of feelings and tastes, a related identity, as well as (consequently) a rudimentary critical discourse to orchestrate these components into competence. Take, for example, a conventional exchange following the latest rock-your-socks film by Michael Bay.

Citizen A: "How'd you like it?"

Citizen B: "It sucked."

Here A asks for B's opinion. A asks how B felt about the film. B expresses his/her experience not as a feeling about the film but, specifically, as a judgement. Sensation has been annexed to value. Behind the confidence of the judgement is, at very least, nascent aesthetic identity: "I know what I like." Some researchers insist, however, that conscience can be active or dormant. A dormant conscience may remain snoozy for the entirety of someone's life, if the person faces few moral dilemmas that "elicit moral conflicts" (Terwogt *et al.* 217) to provoke him/her into moral reasoning. Moral reasoning, provoked by a dilemma, is often what brings about the orchestration of affect and identity, the moral competence without which conscience does not form. The only reason some people (might) have no aesthetic conscience is that aesthetic jargon is less commonplace than moral jargon. Challenges to conscience in the form of dilemmas wrestle the subject into modes of reasoning that might be unfamiliar. To whatever ends, reviewers of poetry practice this, and (as aesthetics dictate) treat books, especially "difficult" postmodern books, as moral-aesthetic problems to reason through, reason with, or reason against.

Contrary to Kant's reason-led conscience, Koops *et al.* conclude that "moral reasoning in everyday situations is nearly always a form of rationalisation" (7), just as aesthetic reasoning articulates nonverbal responses to stimuli. Aesthetic reasoning is nearly always a form of rationalization of affective experience and/or intuitive judgement, which means its role is often as a discursive buttress to extra-linguistic affective and identitarian responses. As Hegel says, the ideolect of conscience articulates what conscience already knows in identitarian and affective ways: "The content of the language of conscience is the self that knows itself as essential being. This alone is what it declares, and this declaration is the true actuality of the act, and the validating of the action" (396). Yet Hegel is insensitive to the ways that reasoning processes can affect feelings and identity. He is insensitive to the fact that, once emergent, all of conscience's components can be transformed.

Conscience is a dynamic, interactive process that emerges in the relationship between moral affect, moral identity, moral reasoning and moral competence, as mediated by perception of moral atmosphere. Rationalisation follows spontaneous affect or congregation of identity, yes, but even if it only stokes intensity, reason transforms those feelings in a way that embeds an ideological sediment. In subjects, such as poetry reviewers, who have a highly developed ideolect for their deliberations, Koops *et al.* suggest "it may be desirable to go through an analytic process in order to test the outcome of the intuitive process" (Koops *et al.* 8). Moral or aesthetic reasoning may work *against* intuition. Feeling can follow reason. Even a realist aestheticist (an aesthetic philosopher who believes in non-social objective (lawful) bases for aesthetic value that could eventually be discovered and articulated) like María José Alcaraz

Léon admits that "a perception can be the outcome of an argument or a piece of reasoning," that subjects may "rationally motivate an aesthetic judgement" (292). Together, processes of aesthetic conscience can produce dramatically new experiences of the same works, as new discursive frames, new affective modes, or new identitarian principles develop.

Moral Competence

Kohlberg, a foundational researcher on conscience in the field of developmental psychology, characterizes moral competence as "the capacity to make decisions and judgements which are moral (i.e., based on internal principles) and to act in accord with such judgements" (qtd. in Koops *et al.* 6). Moral competence in this formulation refers mainly to the command of a moral discourse. As they do in Kant, in Kohlberg affect and identity perform for maestro reason. Yet Koops *et al.* fatally undermine this notion of competence as the mastery of terms, noting that "in certain situations a higher level of [moral] reasoning does not provide better insights" (8). This observation draws from research into moral reasoning and hypocrisy, which finds that "the same level of moral reasoning can be used to justify contradictory moral judgements" (Olthof 329). Conscience works to masterfully negotiate double (and triple, quadruple, quintuple ...) standards, not singular, universal moral dicta.

A definition of moral competence, therefore, must be capacious enough to account for contradictions in conscience, for its efficacy and adaptability, and must integrate hypocrisy as a persistent feature of conscience[8]. Hegel hints at this when he notes that to be "guilty of ineptitude" (391) is to be immoral. I propose that moral competence is best thought in terms of the ability to orchestrate the different components of

---

8 Conscience structurally favours hypocrisy. "Competence," note, is not an honorific. Excellent moral competence, in some cases, means psychopathy.

conscience so that they act in concert, towards conscionable outcomes. The dominant drive of conscience is towards (or back towards) its own quietude. Conscience wants its peace. Any behaviour is conscionable as long as it does not disturb the peace.

Schiller's notion of "harmonization" of the components is a parallel proposal. If competence is not an honorific, "conscionable outcome" may mean behaviour induced from reasoning (as Kohlberg suggested), or that conscience adapts its terms to admit the behaviour into the realm of the morally acceptable, as suggested above. Either would be the outcome of moral competence, and transport conscience back to its desired quietude. This opens my argument to a major point in Hegelian critique of conscience – the risk of its self-sufficiency. To Hegel, conscience's chief imperative is to be consistent within its own terms. As it reaches its "completed form" (398) it grows increasingly self-referential, turned inward, away from the risky world. To Hegel, the "beautiful soul" is a monster of subjective self-projection, a narcissistic psychopath who destroys the universal basis of value, and one that arises from the conundrum of Kant's view that a moral action is one conscientious in intent. Conscience "itself in its contingency [is] completely valid in its own sight, and knows its immediate individuality to be pure knowing and doing, to be the true reality and harmony" (384).

Although conscience never becomes perfectly circular, as impervious to external stimuli as Hegel believes it can be, data reported in *TDASOC* support his critique. Olthof discovered that "children who do bully do not necessarily soften their moral judgements about bullying in order to keep those judgements consistent with their own behaviour" (334). What Olthof unfortunately fails to do is ask these children about their own bullying, for which they may have sophisticated moral rationales[9]. Superlunary beings of conscience, moral virtuosi, can come from

---

9 Arguably, the forms of oppression and domination enacted in bullying are actually imperative under capitalism.

any moral order. Imagine, for example, the patriotic tears of a Bolshevik executioner, as he pulls the trigger of his Mauser for "Russia … first love of the future" (Yevtushenko 488). Despland asks: can conscience be hypocritical? In moral subjects of lower orders – everyone not a moral genius – a competent conscience leaves so much room for hypocrisy that hypocrisy begins to seem to be a central part of the organization of conscience.

Do Not Sin in Tolstoy's Presence

With this brief journey through the chambers of aesthetic conscience fresh in mind, I return to the Yevgeny Yevtushenko poem, to observe his representation of these processes at work in a Soviet citizen.

As Koops *et al.* say, moral dilemmas stimulate conscience. "Individuals ... become acutely aware of implicit conscience-related processes when contemplating, or after actually undertaking, actions contrary to standards" (5). Postmodern poetry frequently presents itself, specifically, as a challenge to standards of poetic conduct, as a moral-aesthetic dilemma. Postmodern poetry is foremost a transgressive matter of aesthetic conscience. Its sense of aesthetic morality is sometimes Nietzschean: "morality [as] nothing other (therefore *no more!*) than obedience to customs ... customs are the *traditional* way of behaving and evaluating" (*Daybreak* 133 emphasis in original). In reviewers' published confrontations with these dilemmas, the processes of aesthetic conscience are traced, with highly varied degrees of aesthetico-moral competence.

Very early in his poem, Yevtushenko names his own Soviet-specific poetic transgression – the stimulant dilemma that unites moral and aesthetic categories. Rather than a categorical challenge, his transgression is a historically myopic flippancy:

> *Superficiality, it is called,*
> *Superficiality, you are worse than blindness.*
> *You can see, but do not care to see.* (480)

For Yevtushenko to have these pangs, he must already have some Soviet aesthetic conscience. Until his crisis, it was either dormant, underdeveloped or less competent. It already knows its unfulfilled duty "for the future:"

> And is not that the reason why we always hurry,
> skimming the surface, perhaps getting down a few inches,
> so that, forgetting courage, we frighten ourselves
> with our task to dig down to the heart of things. (480)

Moral identity often flatters itself that conscience is a positive group-mindedness, a process oriented as much towards others as towards the self, towards some greater collective good, or religious higher good. Such self-congratulatory aesthetic conscience, which presents suffering as a burnt offering get "in good odour with the evil gods" (Nietzsche 130) of a Soviet ideal, is what Yevtushenko's poem describes. "I Journeyed Through Russia" may be a mercy plea to his potential jailers in a highly repressive moral-aesthetic atmosphere. As Yevtushenko is haunted by the crimes and victims of the Tsarist past and capitalist present, his aesthetic conscience develops on an imperative mixture of socialist compassion and Bolshevik pitilessness:

> Let everyone who enters on his life
>   make this promise now
> to help those who ought to blossom,
> and not forget to avenge
> all those who ought to be avenged
> ....
> in the name of righteousness and honour,
> in the name of the establishment of goodness. (481)

Duty and conviction assert themselves. The new aesthetic identity bursts open. After a plaintive, philosophical overture, the poem briefly switches into a more narrative, descriptive mode as the driving tour begins. As the poet and his companion, Galia, motor through the landscape in their Moskvich, Yevtushenko feels "Russia wanted to say something" (482). Russia does so through nostalgic "scents of steppes and birch and pine" (ibid.) which amplify Yevtushenko's shame, until he violently enters the space of this new aesthetic conscience as Russia "thrust our Moskvich into her body" (ibid.).

Russia, now in command, provides her own content to the essentially empty imperatives of duty. "Hearts failing," throbbing with guilt, the two needy "descendents of peasant envoys seeking truth" arrive at Tolstoy's shrine Yasnaya Polyana. Here, compelled by an aesthetic conscience with an underdeveloped ideolect, they fall into a state of reverence. Previously moral affects are transfigured into quasi-religious, aesthetic affect:

> Obeying a silent command
> we entered a shady avenue
> of leaves transparent with sunset,
> named 'Avenue of Silence'.
> And this sheer golden transparency (483)

In this primed state, a baptismal coordination of affect with identity becomes possible. In aesthetic conscience, artistic ancestors often become ghostly chaperones who police aesthetic deeds of the living, the phantoms to whom artists are accountable. For Octavio Paz, that ancestor is Baudelaire; for Peter Bayne, it is Ruskin. To Yevtushenko, the formerly feminized Russia, that so recently could only communicate in nostalgic aromas, merges with a nebulous, enveloping, giant ghost Tolstoy.

> the master of this homestead,
> invisible, kept us in his view,
> and seemed to be present, everywhere around us (ibid.)

The astral body of this "grey-bearded cloud reflected in the lake" (ibid.) of conscience becomes entirely continuous with the Russian landscape.[10] Tolstoy thus transfigures the things of the world, and so establishes the parameters (if not the precise terms) of a new aesthetic discourse that can lead to the harmonisation of conscience: "genius tying the heights and the depths together!" (ibid.). Soaking up into himself, like a Soviet Jesus Christ, the sorrows of all those Yevtushenko says ought to be avenged, Tolstoy's exemplary suffering becomes an aesthetic moral prod:

> was it for nothing that the flame of genius burned,
>   for the sake of changing humanity? (484)

At this stage, Yevtushenko already has a degree of aesthetic moral competence, while the ideolect of his conscience remains underdeveloped: he can't yet articulate the content of the new imperatives. Leaving the shrine, he begins to imagine Russian history almost like an abridged historical slapstick led by "the three greatest names of Russia" (ibid.): Pushkin, Tolstoy and Lenin. The figures who provide conscience its ideolect are therefore part of its content, are among its objects, and are among the phantasms (along with "all those who ought to be avenged" – the suffering masses) to whom it is accountable. When later he "la[y] back the seats" (ibid.) of the Moskvich to sleep, the silent command towards a vaguely imagined justice crystallizes into specific wishes:

> I dreamed of a world
> without the sick and the fat,
> without dollars, francs and pasetas,
> where there are no frontiers, no deceit of governments
> where all the nations are related and in brotherhood (485)

---

10 Yevtushenko's mystical all-encompassing Tolstoy recalls Imam Khomeini's saying: "The universe is God's presence; do not sin in His presence."

By the time Yevtushenko wakes up, the world is transfigured, and there follows a loose catalogue of the ten thousand things of Russian life, aglow in the righteous new light of conscientious duty – full, wakeful aesthetic conscience. Compassionately refusing the "lies in so many tongues" of the outside world, in favour of the Soviet aesthetico-moral ideolect he now commands, he makes an audacious statement that melds identity, conviction, duty and the content of the previous night's dreams (the ideolect):

> *I gladly give away my posthumous paradise,*
> *so that on earth there shall be a little less of hell!* (488)

With his newfound competence, Yevtushenko now judges everything – landscape, history, culture, future – as part of a grand historical pattern, in the correct terms of his well-developed Soviet aesthetic conscience. In this 5000-year plan, Pushkin and Tolstoy historically lead to Lenin, who points to the future "starry night ahead." The poem ends:

> *Pushkin somewhere began to bubble again,*
> *Tolstoy grew more solid, Lenin took shape.*
> *I thought that great enlightenments*
> *were joining together in that redeeming chain,*
> *that maybe is only short of a link? …*
> *Well, what of it, we are alive.*
> > *It's our turn.*

A Retired Engineer Who Reads Houseman and Listens to Recordings of Dylan Thomas: The Tropes of Fantasy

Fantasy and Ideology

The following account, of some of the phantasmic tropes that constitute the dominant reviewing ideolect, is necessary because, as Slavoj Žižek writes, "ideology has to rely on some phantasmic background" (*Plague* 1). In brief, the administrative offices of aesthetic conscience are staffed by a number of phantasms, through whom the reviewer displaces desire onto an imaginary Other. Such displacement, Žižek would argue, more than it teaches the reviewer *what* to desire, teaches the reviewer *how* to desire. To be taught how to desire is, specifically, to set moral limits on what is licitly desirable. To be taught how to desire is also, in effect, to be taught who to be.

To sever his Lacanian concept of fantasy from common sense uses of the term, Žižek establishes a radically anti-common-sensical premise:

> *To put it in somewhat simplified terms: fantasy does not mean that when I desire a strawberry cake and cannot get it in reality, I fantasize about eating it; the problem is, rather, how do I know that I desire a strawberry cake in the first place? This is what fantasy tells me.* (Plague 7)

Licit desire for the correctly determined and validated object (for example, True Poetry rather than Anti-Poetry, strawberry cake rather than blueberry pie) is defined with reference to the imagined desires of an imaginary Other. As often as mercantile reviewers insist on the methodological centrality of the poem-as-such, or the words-on-the-page, a review is rarely about the poetry under scrutiny. A review is about the correct performance of enjoyment or displeasure for a phantasmic audience, and the phantasmic Other(s) governing the reviewer's aesthetic conscience.

Reviewing is predominantly oriented by the ideological need to attract the reciprocating gaze, the approval and subjective confirmation, of aesthetic conscience's governing phantasms. This orientation is crucial to the formation and the hardening of aesthetic identity, since, in effect, in asking them what to desire, reviewers ask their phantasms to tell them who to (aesthetically) be. In late-late-late capitalist culture, consumer desire – sometimes figured as "taste" – indeed often becomes fully equivalent with identity. What I like defines who I am. I am what I want. Dramatizing the scene in childhood, Žižek connects the performance for the Other directly with this formation of identity:

the little girl noticed how her parents were deeply satisfied by this spectacle [of her enjoying the strawberry cake], by seeing her fully enjoying it – so what the fantasy of eating a strawberry cake is really about is her attempt to form an identity ... that would satisfy her parents, would make her the object of their desire. (Plague 7)

In a poetry review the governing phantasms, in addition, have a more determining influence than in other review genres, due to the awkward contingency of its putative object. Žižek addresses the contingency of the external object in general:

the object is reduced to a token which is totally insignificant in itself, since it matters only as the point in which my own and the Other's desires intersect: for late Lacan, the object is precisely that which is 'in the subject more than the subject itself', that which I fantasise the Other (fascinated by me) sees in me. (Plague 9-10)

What matters here is that, in poetry book reviews it is not only the Other that is phantasmic. The token object of scrutiny itself, poetry, where the desires of phantasm and actual reviewer should intersect, is equally phantasmic. Aesthetic conscience needs to establish for ideology, with some precision, the definition or parameters of its object. To the mercantile ideology dominant in poetry reviewing, however, poetry always remains insufficiently substantial to corroborate its own definition, to shore its own limits. Even as ideological tokens, strawberry cakes, paintings, sculptures, buildings, funerary urns, etc., have a substantial objecthood poems do not have. Poetry's ontological condition is something like that of rumour, gossip, urban myth, or language itself; materially traceable (actual) in its social effects, but impossible, for a pointedly mercantile ideology, to substantiate with satisfaction. Poetry is not a thing, but a way of paying attention to language. Poems can only be defined as texts that are read as poems. Furthermore, they are made in the protean medium of language. The need to establish an objective ground for lawful appraisal becomes a matter of renewed crisis in adjudicative poetry reviewing, intensely amplified by the extreme pluralisation of poetic practices (in effect, the de-definition of poetry) since the early 1960s. Before it can pass judgement, before it can settle an aesthetico-moral dilemma, a judging aesthetic conscience has to orient itself in regards to the question: what is poetry? But while conscience can ask that question *of* poetry, but cannot successfully address the question *to* poetry. Poetry cannot speak for itself. That is, in age of a multiply divided poetic field, reviewers cannot discover what poetry "is" by reading poetry. In judgement-driven poetry reviewing, conscience needs from the reciprocating gaze of the phantasmic Other not only a formula of licit desire, and not only consequent identitarian affirmation, and not only the determination of its object, but confirmation of the very existence of its object. The phantasms not only embody aesthetic law in their desires, but establish the only possible ground of adjudicative objectivity: the definitional terms of the object itself. Personified fantasy tropes, mutable phantasms of the Other therefore become inordinately powerful in the aesthetic consciences of Canadian poetry reviewers.

Of the numerous constitutive tropes of fantasy I could examine, I choose mainly those that appear furthest removed from the sensory site of an encounter with a text. (Please note again that in analyzing specific reviews in this book I rarely make claims about a reviewer's other works, and nothing I write here should be taken as personal or ad-hominem.) Among the tropes I neglect, or only glance at, are: the agonizingly Absent Ideal, backroom Career Conspiracies, prophecy of Career Trajectories, the perpetual Crisis of CanLit, the banshee of the Death of Poetry, the mysteriously ubiquitous Everyday, the worried Nation, the longed-for fountain of Posterity, the anxiety of Objectivity, the attentive literary World Audience. As stated, it is the fantasies of readership, the phantasmic Other(s), that most powerfully orient the poetry book review. Most of the recognizably distinct, dominant phantasmic readerships – the Grandparental Reader, the Ideal Reader, the Lost Audience, the Ordinary Reader, the Sensible Reader, the Serious Reader, the Reader Hard to Please – fit, for the purpose of this analysis, under the ordinary umbrella of a Common Reader. In Canadian poetry book reviews, the Common Reader plays the same governing role as Leo Tolstoy's ghost does in Yevgeny Yevtushenko's aesthetic conscience. While far less mystical in conception, and less-all-seeing, the Common Reader is the phantasm to whom the Canadian poetry reviewer is most often accountable in aesthetic conscience.

The fantasized desires of a Common Reader tell the reviewer precisely what is legitimate to desire in poetry, set the terms of aesthetic morality, and prescribe (often retroactively) which compositional practices are licit. The latter frequently serves as a definition of poetry. Steve McCaffery in his rebuttal to Bruce Serafin in *Books In Canada*, is angrily repulsed by this Reader. Where reviewers most often stand up to defend the unitary desires of their conscience-governing phantasm, McCaffery instead defends the concrete heterogeneity of actual reading individuals. Protecting the consumer rights of nonexistent phantasms can, indeed, be taken as an affront to living persons:

To appeal, as he does, to "the common reader" is to appeal to nothing but a judgmental and falsifying term that involves the promotion of a pseudo-consensual essence that does not exist in reality. In a blunter phrase, it is a hollow slogan that insults the heterogeneity of individuals. Who has the right to generalize on quotidian habit? ("Rebutal [sic]")

More defensive moves like McCaffery's are needed in Canadian poetry book reviewing. The Common Reader is so influential that reviewers often silently construct this phantasm as poetry's sole legitimate addressee. In this very context, reviewers frame many formal strategies, contents and subject matters as illicit poetic desire. For example, a traditional illicit desire (or content) in Canadian poetry is "the political" – an expansive derogatory category that can include racialized writing, feminist writing, socialist writing, or overtly justice-oriented postmodern poetry. What counts here is that the political is often constructed as alien to the domain of True Poetry. In a moral word, politics are poetically extramarital. As Stuart Newton writes: "Unfortunately, at the present time, Can Lit has fallen into an affair with politics" (Rev. of Marlatt and Colombo 2).

Wherever there is a disavowal of politics or ideology, as there so often is in poetry reviews, the dominant ideology re-asserts itself into the emptied space of that disavowal. To disavow ideology is to declare yourself its prisoner. The politics that do emerge in reviewing by the 1970s are therefore often a form of consumer-democratic shopper politics. One of the ideological premises of the cultural dominant of consumerism is that everything on the market is, in principle, available to everyone value-free – you only need enough money to buy what you want. In a systemic sense, it therefore insults the pseudo-democratic Common Reader if the poet appears to not write for a (phantasmic) Everybody. By the moral terms of the marketplace, weird or acutely specific poetry smacks as anti-democratic. Reviewing then becomes a form of consumer advocacy, with a notion of Accessibility as its alibi.

Even sympathetic reviewers will affix a kind of "Parental Advisory" label to certain books. As Sparling Mills, author of five collections of poetry, worries: "[Stuart MacKinnon's] decision to use the word 'Mazinaw' as the title of this book could be controversial. Its unfamiliarity might discourage potential buyers" (106). The warning here educates other poets as to the fears, wishes, desires of the phantasmic Common Reader who is, in this case, a nationally projected linguistic subject in the form of a white, Anglophone middle class citizen. Mills' Common (Canadian) Reader knows only one form of English, and shares a common lexicon that does not include the word mazinaw. Common Reader wants the familiar. Or as Douglas Barbour, author of fourteen collections of postmodern poetry and seven books of criticism, cautiously endorses:

These translations are examples of what Nichol has elsewhere called 're-search,' explorations in form (almost pure form; 'content' is not something the authors concern themselves with). In a sense, such writings are intended for limited audiences, but they can prove interesting to any reader willing to try them.... Poets, especially, should find much to ponder about the strictures and structures of formal poetic procedures in its pages, but even the common reader could discover much of interest here. (106)

Barbour slips into a separation of form from content that as a scholar he knows is spurious, or at least indefensible – hence the scare-quotes sheathing "content." Barbour's conscience, however, oriented to the Common Reader, forcibly maintains this provisional discrimination. In his caution that this book is for "limited audiences," Barbour reveals a conventional reviewer's anxiety that if, by chance, the tremulous Common Reader should accidentally encounter the book under review, rather than other imagined poetry encounters, he/she might be scared away from poetry for good. As pictured here, poet-reviewers struggle for the attention (and affection) of the phantasmic Common Reader – who apparently has zero interest in poetry. An unrequited love? As with Mills, the conditioner is what Barbour fantasizes the Common Reader may or may not desire. A normative influence, poetic service to this phantasmic Common Reader curtails critique and exploratory investigation (or "research," as bpNichol called it). These imperatives in postmodern poetry are fantasized as other than what the Common Reader wants. Barbour's distinction, made in good conscience, centres on mimesis, reflection and representation as the licit *raison d'être* of poetry. The customer-is-always-right-wing assumption is that Common Reader prefers homogeneous, comfortably normalized products "stocked with memorable imagery" (Irie 151) like a convenience store.

Crime author Rosemary Aubert similarly issues a product-control supplication to poets, in the form of a caution about the imminent Market Death of Poetry:

[T]he clear, smooth, understandable poem has a definite place in the modern canon. In times when publishers are eschewing poetry in favour of things more 'commercial', it is perhaps time that Canadian poets considered their readers more carefully – not only their readers who are poets and critics, used to reading books with a fine-tooth comb, but also their readers who are members of that hard to please but demanding clique: the general public. Voracious but impatient, the general reader reads to understand and to be pleased. (94)

Aubert's assumption is that most poetry in the "modern canon" – what she believes is the hegemonic dominant of Canadian poetry – is non-Accessible poetry. (Perhaps with exotic titles like *Mazinaw* or insufficient content like *The Kids of the Book Machine*?) Like other reviewers, she constructs this as the reason poetry has a small readership. Encounters with the wrong poetry – the kind most poets write – have scared away otherwise interested readers, which in turn makes publishers invest their capital in other forms of literature. Aubert, as a non-poet, issues this advice with special authority: She is, in actuality, one of the "demanding clique" of Common Readers. When Aubert speaks, the bottom-line (objective) market speaks. This Common Reader has advice for poets: Roll up your mind sleeves; get down to work; say what you mean clearly; say it in familiar language. In this way, poetry might find a profitable niche in the cultural marketplace alongside, say, crime fiction.

Aubert's hesitation over the term "commercial" should also be read in the context of positional antagonisms in the cultural field. Her related assumption is that those same poets, who write with only cliques of poets and critics in mind, suffer their own pangs of aesthetic conscience at the thought of writing "commercial" literature, or worse, a commercialized poetry. Poetry's cultural value has long been constructed through the fantasy of its disinterestedness, the fantasy of Poetry as a virtuously aloof art practice. As Bourdieu writes in *The Rules of Art*:

Even if they are totally opposed in their principles, the two modes of cultural production, 'pure' art and 'commercial' art, are linked by their very opposition, which acts both objectively, in the form of a space of antagonistic positions, and within minds, in the form of schemas of perception and appreciation which organize all perception in the space of producers and products. And the struggles between holders of antagonistic definitions of both artistic production and the very identity of the artist contribute to determining the production and reproduction of the belief which is both a fundamental condition and an effect of the functioning of the field. (166)

Addressing poets as she does, Aubert finds herself in a compromised position. To solve the dilemma, she shifts the definition of "commercial" with scare quotes. In effect she collapses the antagonism between "commercial" and "pure" art. Those quotes reassure poets' aesthetic conscience that literature, and especially poetry, is not really "commercial," regardless of how well (or poorly) it sells. To sell slim volumes of verse is fundamentally unlike selling, say, weight-loss tea. Poets, therefore, shouldn't feel guilty if they want to sell books, nor feel guilty for writing a type of book they expect will sell. At this decadent juncture "it is perhaps time," tsk tsk, for poets to get with the realpolitik program. Otherwise, the poets will kill poetry.

Practically, Aubert's proposed solution to readers' and publishers' decreased interest in poetry is not to build counterpublics (other, specific readerships) or to socially cultivate other modes of reading. Poetry should fearlessly homogenize with other commercial cultural products; it should enter those commercial spaces already available. Poets should feel confident that poetry's pious literariness will hold it aesthetico-morally above any mean commodity. Her underlying assumption about publicness is that it is an extant human quotidian, with a known or knowable, stable set of desires, habits, tastes. But as Michael Warner argues in "Publics and Counterpublics," a reading public "[e]xists only by virtue of being addressed" (50). The Common Reader is fantasized as having a set of given desires cultural producers only need serve. As Warner maintains:

The assumptions that enable the bourgeois public sphere allow us to think of a discourse public as a people and, therefore, as an actually existing set of potentially numerable humans. A public, in practice, appears as the public. (51 emphasis in original)

Certain practical questions might be asked of such assumptions: Where would the Common Reader buy a licit poetry book? Where is the spontaneous encounter with licit poetry supposed to take place? The ideological gap is partially filled by the Canada Council's program "Random Acts of Poetry" through which selected poets are paid to approach to strangers – who perform willy-nilly as the Common Reader – recite a poem to them, then apologize for the intrusion with the consolatory gift of a book of Canadian poetry.

Spreading outward from the Common Reader, the average poetry customer or "even those not used to reading poetry" (Aubert 94), some reviewers construct a more general notion of the Human, towards whom to orient aesthetic conscience. Al Purdy praises Dorothy Livesay for being "a much better and more human poet now ... Livesay is nearly sixty years old now, but I am hopeful ... that this very human poet will go on to another plateau of personal discovery with poems to match" ("Aiming" 88-89). What does it mean to write about a poet or poetry as "human?" In this case, the trope of the Human allows Purdy to accept idiosyncratic poetries, (within limits) stylistically specific to an individual. Human means something like "flawed, vulnerable individual." Human becomes honorific in a generous way: The poetry's most valuable features emerge from conscientious processes like "personal discovery," rather than virtuous, muscular writerly toil. Yet Purdy's equation of "better" = "more human" matters in light of how the fantasy trope of the Human is more often constructed in reviews. The ugly trouble with such a pretty category that it presupposes a harsh definitional limit. Every valorization of specific aesthetic choices as "human" requires, by the logic of discrimination, that others are other-than human. As all desire-orienting phantasms must, the Human valorises certain aesthetics. Its discriminatory negative, however, has a totalizing, quasi-genocidal twang: the Inhuman. There is Human poetry and there is Inhuman poetry. A reader of Inhumane postmodern poetry, by extension, is uncommon, abnormal, perverse, or non-human. Other poetry publics, those not constituted of individual Common Readers, are rendered existentially illicit. (In their critical grasp of this logic, numerous postmodern poets consciously appropriate negative branding in constructing their aesthetic identities, among them: Daniel f Bradley, Christian Bök, jwcurry, Adeena Karasick, Steve McCaffery, and Nathanaël.)

In a review of a book by Marlene Cookshaw, Sharon McCartney, author of three collections of poetry, provides a formula of Human poetry:

the problems confronted are recognizable, and the voice is very human. There are details here I recognise: the mother's distrust of mirrors and tele-

phones, 'desire for flight,' the speaker's refusal to 'be blindly / content with
the elephant's ear,' her wanting the whole elephant. Isn't that what good
writing is about – sounding out our commonness? (105)

McCartney here performs a familiar gesture of pseudo-transparency.
She appears to lay her wish-cards on the table: Familiarity, recognizabil-
ity, centred voice, family bonds, quotidian detail and furniture of the
everyday, operatic and/or soft rock registers of affect, a sense of universal
togetherness. The question is: What does this roster of features propose
as the criteria of Human poetry? Good poetry and Human poetry are
explicitly equated. That "very human" voice, made so by the things it
speaks of, make it "good writing." More than these, the question of read-
er self-recognition is paramount: "problems … recognizable;" "details
… I recognize;" "our commonness." As elsewhere, this is euphemistic
for the consumer narcissism that arises from socially commanded con-
structions of consumer desire as identity. (The clothes make the man.)
In effect, inverse complaints about poetry being not Accessible are often
alibis for impatience with a text that isn't about me. "Where am I in all
this? How does it address me?," these questions, so often asked of po-
etry are questions no reviewer would ask of, say, sculpture. A sculpture
wouldn't be judged bad sculpture because it isn't a bust of the reviewer.
Such self-recognition is, however, often the key criterion of a Human po-
etry. As Christopher Levenson, author of ten collections of poetry, writes
in a review of the Kootenay School of Writing anthology Writing Class:
"All this begs the question, who is conceived as the audience here?" (135).
The logic of Levenson's question is as economistic as Aubert's. Bourdieu
writes: "the economist assumes [consumer 'desire'] to be a given" (*Rules*
172), whereas poetry in fact produces its public concretely, in the circuit
of address and dialogic collaboration. Poetry written for a ready-made
market/audience, with given Human needs, might as well be dandruff
shampoo.

    Postmodern poetry is often framed in these ways as Inhuman. As the citation from Aubert shows, an artistic blood libel is ascribed to its inhumanity – the ancestral guilt of having triggered or accelerated the depletion of a broad audience for poetry. Reviewers like Rosemary Aubert and Brian Fawcett openly fear that, contrary to historical experience, what does remain of a poetry audience will be definitively frightened away by postmodern poetry. In this phantasmic economy, the Common Reader is the constitutive person-molecule of that Lost Audience, which must now be wooed back to poetry reader-by-reader, reflection-by-reflection. Academia, fantasized as the nefarious source of "the postmodern style" is an uncommon site where the Common Reader, specifically, does not reside. Nothing in Academia will carry the Common Reader's reflection. (This in spite of the high rate of university graduation in Canada.) The categorically challenging language of Academia is an alien language. Jargon is inhuman language. When they adopt this language, academics forfeit their status as Human.

An unusually overt example of such reasoning appears in a review of *A Long Continual Argument,* a book of selected poems by John Newlove. Poet reviewer Rob Taylor, author of the collection *The Other Side of Ourselves,* muses that Newlove "spoke to us as Vancouverites, as Western Canadians," and, most importantly, "as humans" in a mode of "honest communication" in direct antagonism with Jeff Derksen's "mega-syllabic disaster of an afterword."

the only real problem the book has is the inclusion of an afterword by SFU English professor Jeff Derksen. The poor man has clearly been stuck between the university's concrete walls for far too long, as his handful of rather lucent observations on Newlove's writing are buried in nine pages of academic garble … Derksen's presentation at the book launch and screening was all the more frustrating. While reading from his afterword, he would occasionally wander off of his notes and suddenly find himself communicating with the audience like a human being, only to quickly fall back into his prepared spiel. ("Newlove")

Editor rob mclennan's decision to invite Derksen to write this afterword is positionally self-conscious. It is a courageous instance of an editor consciously drawing from a different pot of ideolectical ink, against the available default. Derksen's critical and poetic work consistently avoid the dominant ideolect normally used to construct value for Newlove's work – Essential Canadianness, Individual Voice, the Human, Accessibility, Depth, Craft, etc. – while there is no shortage of Canadian poets who would have written afterwords that enthusiastically reiterate those categories. mclennan's goal may be to help bring together the divided field of Canadian poetry; it might also be to provoke controversy, or to call a truce. Regardless, the rifts in the Canadian poetic field were starkly present at the launch of *A Long Continual Argument*. The screening Taylor refers to was of Robert McTavish's documentary *What To Make of it All?*, in which Newlove's work is embalmed in ideological praise by multiple voices, cooing about the deceased in conventional terms. In this space of possibles, Taylor's response to Derksen is structurally predictable. Derksen's afterword (predictably) challenges the terms (by using alternate ones, not through direct contestation), and Taylor (predictably) reasserts those same terms in response. It is a re-entrenchment of positions defined antagonistically.

Taylor directly repeats some of Bruce Serafin's arguments and gestures above, in a similar positional construction of the Academic versus the Human. Academics are prisoners ("stuck between the walls"), they've shamefully forfeited the gift of native, spontaneous speech ("prepared spiel"), they are exemplar victims of a discursive hazard ("only quickly to fall"), while he reports the discourse type ("academic garble") rather than the propositional content of Derksen's spiel. Taylor's goal is to establish the positional antagonism, which does not require him to engage Derksen's arguments. Unlike Serafin, Taylor makes gestures of sympathy ("poor man"), admitting that beneath the phantasmic projection of the Academic pervert is a "real human being."

A Retired Engineer

As seen above in Yevtushenko's poem "I Journeyed Through Russia," conscience-governing phantasms are sometimes personified in meticulous detail. Early into his 72-page denunciation of Canadian poetry at large, "The Great Disconnect," David Solway, author of over 24 books, opens a window into the smartly retro-furnished living room of his Ideal Reader.

[Al] Purdy is a national icon and [John] Ashbery the long-time darling of the conventicles, so there might be some ancillary if unlikely reason to browse intermittently, but can one frankly conceive of any intelligent middlebrow reader spending an evening with Anne Carson or Jorie Graham in the way that my neighbour, a retired engineer, reads Houseman and Hardy and listens to recordings of Dylan Thomas? Answer honestly. (144)

Solway, who aesthetically identifies as "doubly-marginalized," is among the type of righteous culturists Raymond Williams described as "convinced that they are the sole defenders of art in a hostile world" (37). What often slips by like a grace-note in reviews as "the reader," is here given a full figurative contour; a wraith turned to flesh, emerging from a nexus of imaginary readerships compiling the partially contradictory Common Reader, the Ideal Reader, and General Reader. (Like other reviewers, Solway shifts between figures in the course of a single text, while reliably circling within the dominant ideolect.) This strong personification of his phantasmic Other contributes to the hardening of Solway's aesthetic identity, from where he can more bravely launch his global condemnation of Canadian poetry.

Considering Solway's language more closely, his use of "one" (rather than "you" or "I") implies exclusions, because it implies a specific commonality. Specific commonality (in the forms of coteries, communities, cult readerships, etc.) is a defining socio-geographic feature of the poetic field. The question for Solway, then, is: Who does his commonality of "one" exclude in order to achieve its specificity? The poets he rejects are US and Canadian women. The model poets are white, gentile, UK men: A.E. Houseman, who writes eroticized war propaganda; Thomas Hardy, who writes misogynist social criticism; and Dylan Thomas, the hard-drinking, womanizing, troublemaking, bad boy neoromantic. Given this, what gender and race is "any intelligent middlebrow reader" – the phantasmic figure invited to recognise him/her self as part of the "one" – likely to be? Given Solway's personnel of licit poets, and the broader context of a predominantly patriarchal, Eurocentric, white literary field, the figure of the retired engineer will not present itself to the imagination as feminine, or as non-white. In his fleshing out of the Common Reader, Solway also plainly upholds the masculinist associations of crafts discourse, while "any" signals that his white man's Common Reader is the only reader whose attention counts. Anyone who would read women poets like Jorie Graham or (postmodern) Anne Carson must be pathological, or so socially marginal as to be beneath notice.

What licit social role or political agency does Solway's fantasy imagine for poetry? Poetry is reserved a special, autonomous, elite place. Poetry, and poetic experiences, are part of the amassed wealth of the diligent engineer; a luxury comfort (and explanatory existential soundtrack) for an industrious, wealthy man in his decrescendo. In "The Ideology of Canon Formation: T.S. Eliot and Cleanth Brooks," John Guillory unpacks Brooks' reading of a Donne poem in terms that illuminate the cultural concepts operant in Solway's fantasy:

The 'doctrine' here, that the 'well-wrought urn,' is not just the proposition that the poem is an artifact ... it is rather that the urn belongs to the world of value and not to the world of power ... it is the marginality of values which is both deplored and established by the idealization of literature. There is no other place for this value than the mausoleum of well-wrought urns. (192-93 my emphasis)

Solway's mausoleum is the wealthy retired engineer's living room, a place of contemplative withdrawal, not of productive activity. This is not poetry of the job site, but poetry of a busily productive, privileged early life recollected in late-life tranquillity. Yet something in Solway's conception changes the way reified poetry moves from the realm of power into the realm of value. Unlike the museological reification Guillory critiques in Brooks' trope of the urn, Solway's engineer as Ideal Reader retains bodily traces of the world of power he has mastered and transcended. The idealization at work is not as total. Power becomes value only as it ripens through hard work.

Although elsewhere in Solway's review-essay the language of craft emerges overtly ["artisanal respect" (184); "mutual appreciation of crafts-manship" (184); "poems erected" (184); "mastery" (183); "skill traditions" (183)], by comparison to the humble (yet ubiquitous) craftsman common to other fantasies, the neighbour engineer is an Ayn Randian Atlas. By association, it is a class-upward status revision of the metaphorical theme POET AS CRAFTSMAN up to POET AS ENGINEER – as if graduating from master stonemason to architect. The requisite moral dimensions are found in the traces of labour, and in class ("retired" = successful class ascent) as shaping factors. As with Fred Cogswell's "genuine remaining hardware store" below, the white male engineer's livingroom is a site of nostalgia for morally valorized work. Versus the quaint but still active hardware store, the livingroom of long evenings is haunted with memories of a productive past life, site of a well-earned retreat (just as epiphanic revelations in poems, and other textual pleasures, must so often be "earned"). The retired engineer is, in a sense, the ghost of his own past labours. A crucial value difference here between the hardware store and the engineer's livingroom is in the class position of the fantasy subject: blue collar vs. white collar; labour class vs. managerial class. Fundamental differentials of power. When he underscores that the retired engineer is "my neighbour," Solway places himself (and Poetry) in the engineer's geographical, intellectual, and class proximity. "The underlying sensibility," as David Antin acidly remarked of T.S. Eliot, "is the snobbery of a butler" (121).

The Common Reader

Similar to Solway's construction of his phantasmic Other with reference to a living person, who is forcibly recruited to play a symbolic role, reviewers largely write about or address a Common Reader as if it represents a living person or a concrete social type. George Woodcock, author of over a hundred books and pamphlets, in his reminiscence of Milton Acorn, nevertheless begins to grasp that the Common Reader is a phantasm that serves to orient desire and construct aesthetic identity.

Acorn, who thought himself vox populi, *the voice of the people, was in fact very much the poet's poet. It was the poets who created a special prize for him when* I've Tasted My Blood *failed to win the Governor General's award in 1970. And though on that occasion they named him 'the people's poet', that was more in recognition of his intent than a literal statement about his relation to the people, who bought his books no more than they did those of … other contemporary campus and public library bards.* (102)

When Acorn loses the national prize (to Michael Ondaatje and bpNichol jointly), poets rally to reassure him that he really is of the People by giving him a "People's Poet" award. External consecration can indeed be crucial in the process of maturing an aesthetic identity. As Bourdieu writes in *The Rules of Art*:

the artist who makes the work is himself made, at the core of the field of production, by the whole ensemble of those who help 'discover' him and consecrate him as an artist who is 'known' and recognized. (167)

Acorn is so recognized both by the lofty Canada Council (confirmed by the nomination alone), and by his living peers. Yet the People who make Acorn the People's Poet, for and from whom he formulates his aesthetic identity, are a phantasmic People, whom he has access to only in fantasy. The consecration, the legitimisation, his aesthetic conscience needs most powerfully is withheld. In this context, the GG Award seems to hold a special promise for Acorn of actual concrete access to the living People, to that more needed consecration. In the GG Award shortlist he seems to hear the echo of *vox populi*. Acorn's disappointment is therefore an acute threat to his aesthetic identity – the very kind of threat aesthetic conscience dreads most. His friends understand the type of threat well enough, perhaps from their own experiences of comparable threats. The People's Poet counter-ceremony is therefore performed, as a matter of conscience, to help protect Acorn's aesthetic identity from harm. The incident and the review together show the reciprocating attention of the Common Reader used as an ideological stake, in positional struggles among poets, for the credential of Authenticity. Standing up in a poetry review for the interests of the Common Reader is part of this same competition. In receiving the People's Poet award, Acorn wins the title Most Authentic. His supporters, including Woodcock, appear to judge him so specifically because he is most credulously beholden to his phantasmic audience of the People.

The Common Reader is most often evoked in the simple form of the Reader. Arguably, in the simpler form the trope is more normative. "Common" at least marks a discriminatory intent. In the Reader, because that intent is unmarked, the phantasm is constructed inadvertently as universal rather than merely common. In overt or covert forms, the trope can be most normative when used in praise. Reviewers' promises about a book's Accessibility are indeed often disguised ultimatums related to a Readerly Commonness. As Nathaniel G. Moore praises Jordan Scott's second book: "Failing to appreciate the subtle depth of focus here [in *blert*] may require you to consult your mouth or heart for a pulse or feeling" (Rev. of Scott and Tamaki). Moore's divisive gesture is a vital convention in poetry book reviews. Phatic, ritualistic, position-signal passages like these are the mineral resource of review prose. Essence of the review's use-value, they are the extractable core that is multiplied as quotes on/in book jackets, authors' websites, bios, interview questions, and other paratextuals. As many reviewers do, Moore pronounces his ultimatum in the form of an hyperbolic eruption of enthusiasm. Doing so, he raises the stakes of value judgement, of taste, to the order of Human totality: You cannot be Human (cannot have "pulse," "feeling," cannot be alive) if you do not like this book. The imperative of aesthetic conscience – to universalize its maxims – drives these sharp turns which reviews take from praise of a specific book into encompassing claims about aesthetic judgement.

Yet why does Moore articulate his universalized maxim as an ultimatum? Why is the judgement of *blert* of such dire consequence to the reviewer that those who "don't appreciate the subtle depth of focus" should, in principle, be cast out? The constructions of desire as identity that take place in aesthetic conscience mean that discourses of taste, in consumer culture, are inherently discourses of exclusion. The heat of the expression here is not a sign that Moore believes himself part of a minority and must urgently rally others. It comes instead out of the positive thrill of a discovery Moore believes he makes in his love of *blert*: that he is part of a majority. He overflows with the energy of discovery that he is a real boy, at last included in an aesthetic universality of the Common Reader that confirms his own humanity. Like Aubert above, he discovers that he is the Common Reader, whose own desires form the objective basis of virtuous aesthetic morality. He levels his taste ultimatum at potential dissenters to protect this newfound, ecstatic sense of inclusion and identification. It is a positive expression of enthusiasm that encrypts a negative threat: Anything that compromises this feeling of membership will not be tolerated. In this way, ultimatums of taste inversely embody fears homologous to homophobia, where social difference appears to ideology as an intolerable threat to the subject's sense of inclusion in the order of human social normalcy.

Yet why, in a poetry review, does the possibility of dissent seem a threat intolerable to aesthetic conscience? Moore carefully qualifies his explosive gratitude with the reassurance that, although postmodern, the book does not challenge the Common Reader's current categories of value. *blert* occupies "the middle ground between the pathologically-avant-garde and the post-vulnerable-unguarded in Canadian poetry. Jordan Scott is seeking a truth and clarity" (Rev. of Scott and Tamaki). (Note also how Moore uses the division of the field of Canadian poetry, the fact of the poetic cold war, as a basic organizing concept.) Posing initially as a centrist, an impartial referee who takes the reasonable, "middle ground" of objective, lawful judgement ("truth and clarity"), Moore constructs his proposed third way (as if there had only been two, to which Scott contributes a third, rather than a dynamic, evolving plurality of ways) as the only valid way. Other positions are radical – angrily pathological or feebly effete. In this antagonistic moment, the only valid position to Moore is total identification with objectivity, which is to say identification with the law. As Judith Butler writes, the only valid position is "a passionate complicity with the law, without which no subject can exist" (7). To answer the above question: Moore's conscience is so threatened because without this passionate complicity, his own existence in the poetic field is not guaranteed.

In a much earlier review, J.K. Snyder, an English professor retired from St. Mary's University, gives his assumed Reader no outs:

John Donlan's Domestic Economy *is a remarkable book; one way or another, it will be an important one. No one who cares for or about poetry, especially perhaps, poetry in this country will be disappointed in it; and there is a deep temptation in reviewing it to say only that if you do care you will buy it. (164)*

Snyder raises anxieties of inclusion and guarantee, comparable to, but less grave than, Moore's. The stakes for Snyder are not inclusion in the Human; merely inclusion in the social order of Poetry and Canadian poetic citizenship – which means legitimate participation in the poetic field. Unlike Moore, however, Snyder does not at first register the divisions of the poetic field. His "no one" assumes a unity of interest and history, and a consensus of value that he amplifies to the scale of the nation with his qualification "especially ... poetry in this country." Validating *Domestic Economy* is a vulgar test of moral patriotism that purchases poetic citizenship; liking it is a duty.

Although Snyder constructs Donlan's book as "postmodern," Donlan's (valuable) postmodernism is strictly domesticated to conventional intelligibility (value). The postmodern "intelligence" of the book would not be enough to recommend it if the subject matter, formal devices and emotional range of the poetry were not set within known, licit limits:

Domestic Economy *constitutes one of the most assured, as well as the most beautiful, depictions we have of post-modern Canada; nor is it easy to say which is the more astonishing: the easy command of everything philosophical and cultural that has gone into bringing about the post-modern or the intimacy and immediacy with which the daily facts of life in this country are brought to art.... The effect is an exhilarating release into intelligence and inclusiveness – this is a poetry whose door is always open – without surrendering any of the luminous pleasure that comes from tight formal beauty.* (164)

Whereas Shane Neilson can't decide on which aesthetic offence he should indict Roy Miki, Snyder finds it not "easy to say [what] is the more astonishing" about Donlan's book. Snyder's aesthetic conscience compels him to remind the Common Reader that the "postmodern" of this book is only in its subject matter. *Domestic Economy* never uses formal means that challenge inherited concepts of the poetic. Aware of the division of the field after all, Snyder implicitly constructs a positional argument: Other (actual) postmodern books might challenge values or reading practices. In contrast, "this is a poetry whose door is always open." "Intelligence" needn't unsettle what Stuart Newton called "old ways of understanding." Snyder guilts those intelligent (postmodern) poets who don't leave the door of the House of Language open to the Common Reader. Donlan's poetry exemplifies how "intelligence and inclusiveness" need not be antithetical. The postmodern has absolutely no effect on the book's value categories – as a permamodern book of "depictions" of "post-modern Canada." Form again is constructed as a neutral vessel for expressive message content or mimetic content, not the responsive, dynamic medium indissoluble from content. Snyder's construction of the audience's role as dumbstruck admirer of virtuosity – what is "astonishing" is to witness Donlan's "easy command" – polices this division strictly. Empty form operates as a sign of skill and labour in-of-themselves, on the "luminous," socially autonomous plane of virtuosity. "Tight formal beauty" exists away from politics, social history, struggle, memory – away from the struggles that determine beauty. Away from all that produces the division of the field of Canadian poetry. Away from the very "postmodern" of Donlan's book. Yes, being affirmed, being reassured in these ways, rather than challenged, is an "exhilarating release."

Versus the given, obviously obvious Quality Snyder judges in Donlan's book, at certain argumentative junctures a reviewer may revise or withdraw an initial (pre-rationalized) judgement, because some implication in the work brings him/her to the limits of the licit. Sighting such limits, aesthetic conscience spurs into recuperative emergency retreat. Though aesthetic reasoning is often a mode of rationalisation that confirms an affective judgement previously made, it can also work to modify affect. Vancouver reviewer Lyle Neff, prolific literary journalist and author of three books of poetry, the first of which, *Ivanhoe Station*, was nominated for a Dorothy Livesay prize, reviews my own first book *Ligatures* in 2006.

[Mancini's] first book of poems and poem-like things, Ligatures, *has a friendly-looking tricycle silhouetted on its cover, portending, you'd hope, the kind of avant-gardeism that doesn't depend for its effects on a degenerate erudition, but rather on an absolutely fresh, even child-like, approach to important questions. It's a pleasure to report that Mancini mostly lives up to his trike, coming off usually like a bright Martian inquiring into this thing humans call language, and only occasionally like a grouchy Marxist who has read 20,000 books and got tenure the year Foucault died.* ("Introducing")

A turn to the paratextuals (i.e., blurbs, jacket copy, author bio, press releases, cover image, etc.) for discourse cues is often a sign of a reviewer's difficulty lining up the dominant ideolect with the aesthetic imperatives governing the actual book under review. But Neff tries to achieve something even trickier than alignment: He rather generously tries to construct value for a book in the terms of an ideolect it directly challenges and/or rejects. (Note that I have absolutely no grudge with Neff for his review of my book, and remain grateful for his time and attention. The review interests me in this context for what it reveals about the maneuverings of aesthetic conscience.) A core value trope in Canadian poetry reviewing is the Accessible. Neff therefore reads the tricycle on the cover of my book not as, say, creepy or ambiguous. (It's an empty tricycle, so where's the rider? Kidnapped by Catholic priests or Scientologists?) He reads it as "friendly." With this he swings open the door of Accessibility, of licit subjecthood and poetic desire, into familiar delimitations of the Human normalcy.

To fault an author for being too well-read is incongruous enough, but in constructing my book as Accessible, Neff goes further. Erudition is "degenerate;" sub-human. Antagonistic tropes of the alien are evoked to develop the construction under way: The "bright Martian" is negatively contrasted with the "grouchy Marxist." Marxists are another type of coloured alien, yes, but definitely not the cute little-green-men of golden age sci-fi. The quirkily cute Martian lacks the Queen's English mother tongue, deals with language from the outside, as it were. For Bruce Serafin that quality made Steve McCaffery a Franco-phoney ghoul. Here it aids the purchase of innocence necessary to construct my book as valuable. This un-English Martian is aloof of strugglesome human affairs. Linguistically neutral he is also politically neutral (versus the critical, political Marxist), a scientistic experimenter. Disinterest in this context initially forms the aesthetic innocence that Neff further purchases for my book, in even greater quantity, through the trope of the child. Aesthetic-moral innocence is usually acquired through imagined evidence of hard work. Because very little in my book signifies either writerly toil or Accessibility, to protect *Ligatures* from hostile criticism Neff turns me into phantasmic Human shield for myself. Instead of the hard-earned innocence of the diligent aesthetic worker, he gives me some of the inherent innocence of the unspoilt ("fresh") child. The poetry "lives up to [its] trike." My avant-gardeism is licit, loveable, because, "child like," it demonstrates an innate (unpurchased) innocence, a vulnerability. Who would attack a child?

After these impressive contortions, Neff then effectively withdraws whatever endorsement he has given my "intellectually-distinguished and instantly-remaindered" book on behalf of a Common Reader, the phantasm who captains his aesthetic conscience. The Common Reader is advised against braving this book. The exotic pleasures of this place are advertised, but the titillated Common Reader is turned away at the door:

Mancini['s] typographical insanities and mathematical insults to English aren't just for laughs ... but they also aren't for everyone.... This is not to cut down Mancini's witty and mirthful accomplishment in Ligatures, *but to say that it's a rarefied piece of work, a cunning and esoteric thing, built for connoisseurs.* ("Introducing")

Here the reviewer overtly revises his own judgement (as an actual read-

138

er) in deference to the presumed desires of the phantasmic Common Reader ("everyone"), the Joe Poetry whose interests the reviewer has a moral-aesthetic duty to serve. As Žižek writes: "[F]antasy animates and structures enjoyment, while serving as protective shield against its excess" (*Welcome* 7). Here, the immoral "excess" would be transgression of the bounds of licit poetic desire – Neff constructs connoisseurs who could like my book as arch-perverts.

In other formulations, Slavoj Žižek names the authoritative phantasmic Other, after Lacan, the Subject Supposed To Know. Žižek extends this naming practice in various forms, which indicate how the presumed desires of an Other might be variously imagined in different contexts: the Subject Supposed to Loot and Rape; the Subject Supposed to Believe; the Subject Supposed to Enjoy; the Subject Supposed to Know. Neff's Common Reader, Canadian poetry reviewers' Common Reader, is often the Subject Supposed to Not Know. In other manifestations he/she is: The Subject Supposed to Not Buy Books. The Subject Not Supposed to be Burdened. The Subject Not Supposed to Not Want to Be Challenged. Sometimes, he/she is the Subject Supposed to Be Easily Made to Feel Stupid. Neff confesses that he likes *Ligatures*, but does not believe the Subject Supposed to Not Know could possibly like it. Although the actually existing reader Lyle Neff likes *Ligatures*, Lyle Neff's aesthetic conscience predictably condemns the book, after a show trial of due process. Common Sense Cop reviewer protects the vulnerable Common Reader from a threatening encounter, while the rigours of adjudicative duty prevent the reviewer from slipping into an irrational (degenerate, perverse – "witty and mirthful") postmodern exuberance of approving a strange book.

Similarly, Norbert Ruebsaat, teacher and author of the collection *Cordillera*, writes in an open letter review of Robert Kroestch's *Completed Field Notes* in 1990:

So, Robert – congratulations. I liked your book as a writer; I dislike it as

a reader. Or: I like the book as reader, as text written from you to me,
but as Reader (some kind of public individual/purchaser of books) I was
thrown off and/or bored by it. What does Barthes call it – lisible versus
scriptible. *Yet there's something compelling about this. Freeing up the text:*
finding other forms. [Certain sections] of Kroetsch's book ... work because
I don't read them as 'poems'.... But a disappointment enters the moment I
demand they be poems as well: that they answer the question: why are we
in this book, as well as stating the demand: read me. (120)

Whereas Neff projects this Common Reader "everyone" entirely out-
wards, as if it is a concrete social type, Ruebsaat knows that the readership
is an internal construction. Ruebsaat grasps that he is, like any critic, at
least two readers (two aesthetic consciences) in one. He is a split reader.
He does not, however, quite grasp the Common Reader as a phantasm
of ideology. Quite beyond the fact that poststructuralist concepts are in
wide circulation, Ruebsaat suggests he has read Barthes in the original
French. Yet he chooses not to draw from this other, commensurate ide-
olectical pot of ink, and addresses Kroetsch's poetry in terms that he is
consciously aware it directly rejects. The dominant Canadian Common
Reader is in command of this aesthetic conscience, and Ruebsaat fears
loss of the phantom master's attention if he changes his ideolect.

One particularly hilarious form of the Common Reader is often
seen: the Grandmother Reader. Among reviewers, her wise, endearing
phantom is normally evoked with some form of the question: "What
would my grandmother think of this poetry?" Production side, she is
evoked by poets as giving aesthetic imperative: I want to write poetry
my grandmother would understand. In the same review of *blert*, Moore
jokes about the Grandmother as Common Reader trope, without fear of
the allusion being missed:

if you're into straight-forward traditional Canadian poetry, (Raffi, Anne
Murray, Air Supply, Gordon Lightfoot) or want your narrative spoon-fed

*to you through a reed-straw whilst slowly having your muffin buttered by
one of your grandmother's friends, you might want to leave Blert at home.*
(Rev. of Scott and Tamaki)[11]

In light of Moore's earlier validation of *blert's* aesthetic "middle ground"
between the wacko-garde and weepy-garde, a book the Common Reader
need not fear, this passage represents a somewhat dissenting turn. Now
he warns a different Common Reader (one like Lyle Neff's) away from
the book, but in such a way that he *de facto* reformulates, based on his af-
fective responses to *blert*, his own Common Reader. He contests formu-
lations like Neff's with his own middle-pathological phantasm. In effect,
he asserts that the governing Common Reader, poetry's legitimate ad-
dressee, should not be the Subject Supposed to Be Totally Brainless and
Easily Frightened he sees constructed elsewhere. The question that still
dangles is: What danger or risk ("leave it at home") does Moore intuit?
The danger may be that in reading an unconventional text the Common
Reader phantom will discover he/she has no reflection.

Žižek's Lacanian-Marxist model of ideological fantasy explicitly an-
ticipates the mutability of persistent tropes like the Common Reader.
Similarly, the theory of aesthetic conscience anticipates the individual-
ized reformulations and impletions of fantasy tropes and the potential
variety of ideolectical terms. And so, the often imperfect distinction
between forms of phantasmic reader, and reviewers' tendency to swing
promiscuously between tropes of Ancestral, Ideal, Common, Sensible,
Ordinary, Average, Everyday, General, Grandparental Readers. While
this is certainly an effect of the self-protective inventiveness of con-
science, Žižek argues it can be understood with reference to sexuality:

---

11 All of his examples of "traditional Canadian poetry" are, oddly, drawn from music,
not literature. Is Moore right to suggest that the affective paradigm of Canadian
official verse culture is best represented, in some hybrid way, by the music of Raffi
and Air Supply?

This role of fantasy hinges on the fact that 'there is no sexual relationship',
no universal formula or matrix guaranteeing a harmonious sexual rela-
tionship with one's partner: because of the lack of this universal formula,
every subject has to invent a fantasy of his or her own, a 'private' formula
for the sexual relationship – for a man, the relationship with a woman is
possible only inasmuch as she fits this formula. (Plague 7)

In aesthetic terms: There is no aesthetic relationship. There is no cor-
rect, aesthetico-moral relationship for aesthetic conscience to aspire
to. Consequently, each reviewer must assemble his/her own formula.
A reviewer, in particular a severely adjudicative one, works out in aes-
thetic conscience a custom formula of standards of appraisal, which
are predominantly figured as the assumed desires of the Common
Reader.

Steve McCaffery poses the question above: by what authority does
any reviewer presume to speak for a Common Reader? His question
could instead be: How do reviewers arrive at their specific formulations
of the desires of the Common Reader? Some reviewers plainly univer-
salise their own reading responses, or their particular cultural literacy, as
the human common denominator. In effect they are electing themselves
as the standard of human normalcy. This is the passionate complicity of
reviewer with Common Reader as the bearer of aesthetic law. If ideology
and habit sometimes make it easy to pass smoothly over these aesthetic
universalisms, one trips over their hard limits where untenable class as-
sumptions or positional assumptions poke up. In the same review cited
above, Rosemary Aubert writes:

For the average middle-class reader, this book is like a glimpse through the
window into a kind of home one has heard about but never seen, though
that home is as likely the streets as it is to be run-down rooming house
room…. 'A Special Occasion' is an apt, funny, tragic vignette of life in an
inner-city, inelegant apartment building. Anyone who has ever lived in,

*or even visited, such a building will recognise it at once…. [Plantos'] book
presents a viewpoint, a voice, from within a usually silent crowd.* (95)

In Aubert's formula, the Common Reader of Canadian poetry is the "av-
erage middle-class reader," to whom Plantos' book provides an opportu-
nity to be a poverty-tourist Peeping Jane. Her invitation to take a walk on
the inelegant side is supported with eyewitness testimony, because she
anticipates her white, middle-class Common Reader's incredulity that
some kinds of people actually live this way. More titillating is that these
kinds of people (the poor – and implicitly First Nations people), who live
in these kinds of shabby homes, actually write poetry. They even have "a
voice." Who knew? Do they have a language? Might it include the word
mazinaw? Where she writes "silent" Aubert may have written "invisible,"
redacted by ideology.

Whether or not Aubert's assumptions have demographic validity,
compelled by structural forces far broader than the mercantile pressures
of the review genre, she has demonstrably internalized the corporate
concept of people and populations, who constitute a market with given
desires cultural producers have the duty (and honour) to fill. As a de-
mographic market entity – statistics with a human face – do not think
of the reviewer's *we* or *one* as Royal or collegial. The reviewer's *we* is
the Common Reader, when the reviewer explicitly includes him/herself
in that group. (In these cases, the identification can sometimes take the
form of an expression of solidarity with the Common Reader against an
offending poet, as if taking up a position with the whole swarming mass
of a phantasmic humanity against a hated outcast.) As poet Stephanie
Bolster, author of four books, including *White Stone: The Alice Poems*
which won a Governor General's award, writes:

*When I jokingly characterise the quintessential Canadian poem, to my stu-
dents, as a first person domestic lyric – perhaps involving the washing of
dishes by a window outside of which weather occurs – am I describing not*

what is written but what certain editors prefer? When I consider my own poems of this kind – of course I write them – throwaways, what possibilities am I curtailing? We all know that trying to be original rarely results in true innovation. Perhaps the best way to truly reflect the culture out of which one writes is not to think about that culture. But to do that, one has to trust that the culture lies firmly under one's feet. ("Surviving")

Her reassurance "of course I write them" is a chirp from a perturbed conscience. Aesthetic conscience is (rightly) pricked with fear that antagonistic questions (i.e., critique) will harm, disturb, or destroy, the very discursivity (the ideolect) that constitutes it, so it sounds a self-interpellative distress signal: Come back to yourself. Bolster thus tacitly admits that the introspective processes of quintessential Canadian poetry are categorically circular, as Hegel warned of conscience, because critique of its devices, practices or categories poses an existential threat – the circle might be broken. The ideal Canadian poet therefore would not ask questions, would not think critically, would simply channel a quintessential Canadianness through a highly competent aesthetic conscience. Bolster hedges again, however, nervous that this dish-washing, weather-watching middle-class subjecthood is not (yet) securely universal. The trope therefore shifts from culture as pre-given ideology ("out of which one writes" – into what?) to culture as something that must be obtained. Once obtained, culture, at last, "lies under one's feet" as after a journey and/or self-interpellative process of acquisition.

Accessibility

As it functions in reviews, Accessibility is rarely a trope of reading comprehension or interpretation. Accessibility is a fantasy spatial trope of text-reader relationships, figured in reviews through a variety of spatial-relational analogies. Sometimes the analogy is of a text-to-reader embrace: An Accessible text figuratively "embraces" the Reader. Most often the analogies are architectonic access-points: entranceways, gates, doors, arches. From these, it seems that the underlying fantasy is of poetry as a special place to visit, clearly separated from quotidian territory by sometimes enchanted portals. An assertion is projected, also, that the Common Reader desires active, direct involvement in what goes on in that special place. Yet the specific forms of the aesthetic demands made through the trope Accessibility, in the name of the Common Reader, presume only passive reception. An actual demand for narcissistic passivity is made through the trope of Accessibility in the form of a demand for active participation. If Accessible poetry is a special place to visit, reviewers righteously demand the Common Reader be given a guided tour of that place.

As poet Stuart Newton writes, in a review of books by Mona Fertig, Henry Rappaport and Edwin Varney:

The use of stream of consciousness to break down old ways of understanding tends to leave the reader out of the experience. The images carry hints of sharp and painful edges, like a knife, but the feelings remain somewhat ambiguous. (142)

A notable parallel construction is set up here between "the reader" and "the experience." "The reader" is constructed (in fantasy and in actuality) out of old categories, "old ways of understanding," that poetry must re-affirm in its representations. The experience, supposedly, is not of the poem itself, but vicariously of the experience the poem represents. A "stream of consciousness" poem intended to provide a unique experience, rather than represent an experience, is unintelligible because the actual reader cannot so easily find the *look-dad-it's-me* confirming effect of subjective reciprocation (i.e.,"tends to leave the reader out" of the picture).

Newton's second sentence formulates some stylistic requirements of Accessibility: A poetry is Accessible if the emotions it invokes are of a broad-contoured kind[12]. Subject matter (which the poem must have, first of all) has to be familiar or made to feel familiar by its affective envelope. When these demands converge to produce a phantasmic Poet persona, subjectivity itself can become the Accessible place to enter. Does the poet let readers into her feelings? Will Dirty Harry (deconstructed or reconstructed) let his cute new Asian girlfriend into his heart? As so often reiterated by L=A=N=G=U=A=G=E poets: the trope of Accessibility demands passivity in the inverted form of a demand for active reciprocity. An explicit rejection of the (reader-empowering) view of texts as co-constructions of reader and writer, Accessibility presumes the poet does all the construction work, after which the reader just walks on in – provided, naturally, that the gates of the House of Language are not locked.

If poetry shouldn't "break down old ways of understanding" at risk of losing its categorical status as poetry – true Canadian poetry is Acces-

---

12 His muted demand for sharper delineations of feeling recalls what Antonio Gramsci called the "operatic conception of life," and "operatic taste" in literature: "the operatic appear[s] as an extraordinarily fascinating way of feeling and acting, a means of escaping what [is considered] low, mean and contemptible [in life] … to enter a more select sphere of great feelings and noble passions" (373).

sible – what social role does this grant poetry? One much like Bolster's above. Criticality, doubt, uncertainty – important registers in postmodern poetry – make feelings ambient, indefinite or microscopically specific, non-operatic, vexing. With the certainty of a solid cultural ground under one's feet, poetry instead works reflexively, expressively to act as a social, cultural, affective guarantee. Poetry should be an ideal mirror to flatter consumer narcissism and aesthetic conscience.

Determinations of factors such as emotional intelligibility or familiarity of subject matter can only be made as projections that universalize a particular aesthetico-moral formula. Accessibility, like the Human, can raise the moral ante by framing these particular-universal limits as the very bounds of normal, healthful literary competence. While vagueness is a problem for a reviewer like Stuart Newton, emotional abnormality, or emotions not of the operatic kind, just as often make poetry Inaccessible to a reviewer. All that exceeds or dodges these limits is pathologised. If the Accessible is poetry servicing the libidinal needs of a normative Common Reader, anyone who can pleasurably read Inaccessible poetry is the threatening Uncommon Reader, beyond the healthy limits of literacy, thought to be perverse. Anyone who can read the Inaccessible is cognitively abnormal, and/or stands on a different, alien cultural ground.

Conversely, Accessible poetry is poetry "whose door is always open" (Snyder 155). In the context of domestic myth and minutiae, the poems that someone like Michael Ondaatje writes "are accessible to anyone who wants to try – he doesn't alienate his audience but seduces them into that privacy" (Musgrave 194). In contradistinction, a reviewer (identifying with/as Common Reader) might feel that he/she "remains outside of the circle of friends" (Aubert 109) of a poet, or even becomes a victim of its textual cruelties, its heartless inaccessibility. As Wayman Chan writes of Brian Henderson's book *Year Zero*:

I yearn to interact with these written words, yet I'm somehow shut out cleverly.... Henderson takes us away from the emotional trappings of flesh

towards the theory of generative enslavement.... Again I'm shut out by
paradox, sleight-of-hand, waiting at the doorstep of Master Language. (84)

A further point to notice in Chan's review is the total identification of the Accessible with Poetry itself. If Chan is "shut out" by the verbal play in Henderson's poetry, this poetry has no "inside" to get into. Un-enterable (Inaccessible), it is not poetry. It is the exclusive House of Language, a set of walls without an interior room. Chan's protective discourse here acts to shield the Subject Supposed to Be Easily Made to Feel Rejected from an encounter with the unpredictable emotional swerves, the ambiguous emotional paradoxes of Henderson's illicit, immoral ("sleight of hand") text.

The Human

When Canadian poetry reviewers use the words "humanism" or "humanist," the term is normally set in implicit or explicit confrontation with a poetics deemed Inhumane. (Negative evocations of these tropes have a negative position-signalling function: This is where I am not.) As Linda Sandler writes:

I suggest also that [Irving] Layton's self-advertised pole-vaulting heroism is a parasite, feeding on his sense of belonging to a persecuted race – and that coarse rhetoric is not convincing as humanism or as poetry. (94)

Humanism here is not a gesture towards the historical, philosophical meanings of the term – neither a Renaissance humanism of classical learning, nor the later secular appropriation of the term in the name of reason as the guiding power of a progressive history. In poetry reviews, humanism usually means something like "the quality of humanness," referring to affects considered constitutive of the Human. So humanism here means something like an affection for the paraphernalia of culture, and a belief in refined operatic feeling (versus "coarse rhetoric") as the highest form of poetic praxis. Humanism is furthermore a demonstrable acquiescence to the terms of Accessibility. Poets can signal their Humanity by various lexical means, by deploying a relatively fixed lexicon of "poetic" words, or by showing a tenderness towards the furniture of the ubiquitous mysterious Everyday. Further, the overarching goal must be affective intelligibility: A humanist poem makes some part, small or large, of experience more affectively intelligible, more narratively coherent than it was before. Margaret Harry, formerly an associate professor of English at St. Mary's University, in a review of books by Tom Wayman and John Lent, draws the contours of this humanism:

The fragmentary thoughts and images that move through his mind are matched by a deliberate fragmentation of form. Within the chronological framework of the sequence is detailed the clash between the ephemeral observations of a mind partially occupied with the sub-intellectual business of driving or sitting at a roadside café and the highly literate enclosing context; and entangled in this primary conflict is another, where the poet is caught between the triviality of contemporary reference and the ungrasped, timeless reality of the lake, the trees, the road. (74)

Note how the first sentence partially decouples form from content. How could the "thoughts and images" be fragmentary in of themselves if they were not fragmentary in form? Yet they are only "matched by" formal fragmentation. "Deliberate" marks a hesitation about licit poetic desire, as if it is so radical and/or strange and/or new that a poet writes in fragments (as late as 1983!) that the Common Reader needs to be forewarned that it is not unintentional. The "enclosing context" is "highly literate" because made up of items from the "timeless order" (world as discourse and synecdoche), contrasted with the sub-literary features of "driving" and the "roadside café." Here the contemporary (the not-timeless, the timeful) is "trivial," which signals for the reviewer a dramatic drop in brow-height, while other "timeless" items are poetic, high-brow. The road – a more recent invention than trees or lakes – was presumably also "trivial" to poetry reviewers of the ancient world, but with the Roman Empire and, later, global car culture, it has joined "the lake [and] the trees" in Nature. Harry's dubious central dichotomy is exactly Fredric Jameson's dubious dichotomy: The postmodern as an empty play of surfaces versus the modern as a plumb of Human depths.

To be fully Human, however, poetry almost necessarily has to seem to come from a discernible subjective somewhere – that place one can enter if the door is (wide) open – specifically, it has to express a poetically licit persona. It has to be centred in a phantasmic Poet who desires to speak to the Common Reader. As Sharon McCartney writes: "Poetry is not fiction; it's not enough to simply tell a story. We have to be able to identify a speaker, a 'someone' whose voice is the reason for the poem" (106). In spite of the relentless (and ongoing) pluralisation of poetry in Canada since the early 1960s, the lyric remains statistically and materially the dominant paradigm of form and address. Expression, voice, a phantasmic Poet, provide the imperative of this aesthetic conscience – the need, and human right, to say something you mean to say. To write poetry is to write what you know and to say what you mean about what you know to the Common Reader to whom, of course, you want to say it.

In contrast with the Common Reader *we*, the reviewer's *us* extends further outward to become a conceptually vague, more total trope of Humanity. Through *us*, the *we* gesture becomes a universal embrace. If the Human in some ways represents a wish for universality, remark how often this Human is evoked with highly specific, culturated forms and markers of domesticity – washing dishes after supper in the suburbs, for example. It extends from a naturalization of specific forms of Canadian consumer life, and a universalization of class-specific experience and paraphernalia. Just as for Rosemary Aubert's Average Middle Class Reader, for Don Precosky life is homogenous, and safe: "We are voyeurs, parasites vicariously drawing meaning from the safely distanced tragedies of others as they are served up to us in convenient bites on radio and television" (113). The Common Reader's life is a space of a (mildly) turbulent domesticity "the domestic jungles we inhabit so clumsily" (McCartney 105). Here poetry is a balm, a comfort, a medicine and guarantee: "The 'little epiphany' here is something we all know—that music, indeed all art, is food for the soul" (Shreve "How Poems Work"). This is the specific Human content, the familiar subject matter and mould of experience, that makes poetry Accessible.

The Postmodern

What reviewers construct as the Inaccessible in postmodern poetry makes Difficulty, again, more relational, and sometimes more discriminatorily sinister, than an interpretative, communicative or qualitative quandary. Inaccessibility, as the concept relates to the Common Reader and the Human, does not merely make postmodern books bad poetry, or non-poetry. It is among categories invoked to put books under review beyond the fray of the Human. Inaccessible poetry, like jargon, is inhuman gibberish. (A person without conscience is a psychopath. A poet without aesthetic conscience, i.e., one who would write such poetry, is similarly monstrous.) Outside the politics of recognition and poetics of guarantee – mimesis, reflection, the Accessible – the Human is unrecognizable. Among the terms that often signal the reviewer has detected the inhuman postmodern is "cynical." Cynical poetry lacks the normalized (as above) signs of feeling that constitute the fantasy Human; its gaze is "cold," it is sneeringly Difficult, or leaving the Common Reader on the chilly doorsteps of language. Stylistically, poetry described as cynical often lacks the safely rapturous tone of the pre-loved beautiful, or does not draw from a (surprisingly specific) poetic lexicon of the natural/timeless or the bourgeois/domestic. Other forms of textual pleasure, and other reading practices, are illegitimate or – in a deleterious, homophobic sense – queer. A crossover figure like poet Erín Moure[13] can have

---

13 As well as many others, such as Elizabeth Bachinsky, Garry Thomas Morse, Phil Hall and Wayde Compton.

structural importance in the divided field, because her work appears to many reviewers, in certain senses, to meet the demands of the Accessible, while signalling postmodern sophistication in other ways. Leona Gom, author of six books of poetry, celebrates Moure's writing because

even when the poems don't quite work, when they leave you with a sense of having missed too much, they are still rewarding.... Image builds on image, detail on detail, always appearing effortless, the craft beautifully absorbed into art ... there is a recurrence of themes of loneliness, violence, injustice – it is a look at life's hard edges, but this is hard-edged poetry. And if there is cynicism, there is also a strong core of humanism, of caring about this world and the people in it. (147)

An antagonism between the cynical and the Human is set up directly, followed with a fairly succinct definition of what reviewers usually mean by humanism. The use of the "core" suggests (correctly) that humanness is a "sense of," a "feel," a certain poetic affect constructed through a conventional set of signifiers of "caring." Gom's "you" becomes very much a reviewer's *us*; with a phrase like "having missed too much" she enlists herself in the army of the Common Reader. The Accessible tends to demand that poetry make a performance of full disclosure on the first encounter. In its use of new lexicons, its address of a community rather than a crowd, its valuation of the particular (or cryptic), this disclosure is one of the things postmodern poetry is believed to withhold with ulterior ("cynical") motives. Postmodern poetry doesn't say what it means or relate (in operatic terms) what it feels – this is why it is "cynical." Gom warns that some of Moure's poems will give the Common Reader that (presumed) experience of cruel exclusion, which is to say Moure's work has some "cynicism," where it refuses to show the Common Reader his/ her own reflection. In Gom's defence of Moure as, nevertheless, a Human poet, lurks the xenophobic, crypto-racist construction of other postmodern poets as psychopaths without feelings – monsters with no aesthetic conscience, as Nietzsche said.

In a review by Don Precosky (prolific reviewer, editor, and former Dean of Arts and Social Services at the College of New Caledonia) of Sharon Thesen's *Pangs of Sunday* and Barbara Carey's *the year in pictures*, he returns to the notion that without religious belief human life is meaningless, nihilist, abysmal and cruelly mute. Poetic postmodern cynicism is an effect of the loss of this core desire for a return to "traditional meaning," in whatever form. Precosky laments that these poets

present an all-too-accurate description of what life is really like for most people today ... most of us don't really believe that there is a power that moves through all things ... an electricity waiting to be plugged into. A lot of our poets now place that power in 'Language,' but it's rapidly becoming apparent that that particular pudding is not very good eating and that a lot of our postmodernist poets sound like each other and are all becoming boring ... [In Thesen's book] the day of rest gives rise to pangs because of its emptiness first, of routine, and second, of traditional meaning. We are supposed to stop the daily grind of things to do something special – to celebrate our connectedness with a higher power. When that belief in the connectedness is gone then rest turns to 'pangs.' (115)*

A number of postmodern poets did shift capital L-Language from a productive compositional trope into a quasi-mystical god-term, bpNichol not least among them. Yet Precosky sounds the common complaint that language is not sufficient for poetry, that language is not what makes poetry "good eating." The good eating is found in what language can signify beyond itself, arising from language's mimetic, or even instrumental capacities. Subject matter can assure a reviewer that the poetry under review is not bloodless, gutless, or godless – that it is Human poetry. So postmodern poetry is a symptom of the very afflictions suffered by "most people" in postmodern times, its blood (belief) drained away until it becomes "boring" (dead). He regrets the loss of social connections that tradition, in the good old days, supposedly provided. Godful lyric poets – or let's say agnostic-with-cravings lyric poets – are quasi-priestly healers. All that might be left to these medicinal poets to do is find "that power" in the experiential bric-a-brac of Average Middle Class Reader's domesticity, or perhaps to twine the religious with the poetic in such things as the "timeless reality of the lake, the trees, the road," as per Margaret Harry.

Academia

Academia is a fantasy site that functions as an antagonistic spatial trope in the discourse of the Human. Academia is the fantasy place the phantasmic Common Reader dare not, or cannot, enter. Much of what reviewers identify as Inhumane in postmodern poetry – in particular, its alleged concern with things theoretical or cerebral rather than the "emotional trappings of flesh" – originates in this equally phantasmic Academia. As Greg Gatenby, author of four books of poetry, writes in a review of *Death of a Lady's Man* by Leonard Cohen, the Academic is an insult to normal reading practices, to normal habits of feeling and cognition, a threat to healthy normalcy:

From there he moves to the kind of commentary tendered by especially sententious doctoral students, and ultimately so confuses the reader with his shifts of tone that only the perfect insomniac (or his friends – or a harassed reviewer) could fail to put the book down in exasperation by midpoint. (78)

Gatenby makes the key antagonist of the Common Reader the (wannabe) Academic: the pompous graduate student. Where reviewers frequently project a universal Common Reader through "the reader," Gatenby gives a short list of alternate readers, making his Common Reader definitely positional (rather than supra-positional/universal), with antagonists: friends of the author (community as exclusivity); harassed reviewers (reading under pressure); nerdy insomniacs (Academic creatures of the night). His complaint about Cohen's tone makes Cohen's postmodern shiftiness into a positional issue, as well as a sign that the poem is an encryption. "Perfect insomniac" alludes to the putative ideal reader of James Joyce's *Finnegans Wake*, an "ideal insomniac." If "shifts of tone" create the knotty "confusion" that only a Joycean ideal insomniac would have the patience and free time to disentangle, "tone" must be an encryption of what the poet really means to say. Rather than register the shifts as Cohen's playful critique of (and evasion of) definite authorial position, Gatenby judges it a postmodern puzzle. With a familiar adjudicative ultimatum (more common in positive form – "if you don't swoon with love for this book have someone check your pulse") Gatenby takes on what he supposes the Common Reader desires: sure knowledge of what the author means and where the author stands. Common Readers with normal sleeping and reading habits are locked out of an experience designed for their antagonists, the crazy vampire eggheads of the Academy.

Postmodern poetry enters the Canadian poetic field dramatically under the very sign of a malign Academia. Black Mountain College is the name of the legendary U.S. arts college where Robert Creeley, Robert Duncan and Charles Olson taught for several years. Creeley, Duncan and Olson are the paternal figures whose work had such a determinate, openly declared influence on the writing of the young *Tish* group. In the reaction to *Tish* poetics and community politics "Black Mountain," temporarily assumes a token status in poetry reviewers' ideolect, as a shorthand for both bad postmodern poetry and for harmful cultural radiation emitted from the U S A into Canada, mutating Canadian verse forms. This response arguably culminates in book form with Keith Richardson's 1976 *Poetry and the Colonized Mind: Tish*. A few years earlier, Milton Acorn publishes an article in the cultural protectionist vein called "Avoid the Bad Mountain" in *Blackfish*. Acorn writes:

I shall not say Black Mountain this article, but instead say Bad Mountain;

as a comment on what (I think) should be done, and what (I think) should be avoided.... Avoid American models.... So when I say AVOID THE BAD MOUNTAIN, *what I principally mean is avoid Yankee models.... Do not, repeat* not, *try to found a school of poetry. That's why* TISH *was such a disaster area.* (1972: no pagination)

Community is exclusive to others (such as the reviewer), while threatening the fantasy autonomy of Poet self. The apparent incongruity that a devoted communist like Acorn would fear community tells again of an internal split – Acorn's aesthetic conscience and his political conscience diverge. In poetry, unlike in labour relations, an individual *must* go his/her own way. In contrast, for a poetry group to go their own way together – any attempt to "found a school of poetry," which is to say form a coterie who orient to each other rather than to the phantasmic Common Reader – invites poetic "disaster." Academia and community ("school") morph into a common phantasmic object of fear, in a negatively constitutive relationship with the Common Reader. The individualism that underpins the dominant aesthetic conscience often constructs community as threatening in this way, some ideologically unresolved combination of resentment of exclusion and fear of assimilation. As Wynne Francis, after whom Concordia University named an "Award for Excellence in the field of Canadian Poetry Studies," writes of Irving Layton:

The book closes with a poem destined for anthologies. The critics may tut-tut all they like about its sentimentality and its archaic rhetoric, but Layton's public, which ranges far wider than academia, will love every word of it. (83)

Francis' critics are both non-Human Academics (whose language marks their distance: tut-tut) and critics in the vernacular sense: people who are critical, i.e., negative reviewers. To defend Layton, Francis' retort is to literally to evoke the spectre of the massed Common Reader as "Layton's public," wider (more normal, Human) than the narrow reading of academia or naysayers out of touch with even their own humanity. Yet Francis' argument moves this way as if in response to the hurt of a prior exclusion: If you exclude Us just remember we outnumber you 1000:1.

Sarah Ahmed, in "The Economy of Affect," unravels emotional structures of contemporary forms of xenophobia and tribalism that will illuminate these positional constructions of the Common Reader.

This narrative is far from extraordinary. Indeed, what it shows us is the production of the ordinary. The ordinary is here fantastic.... The ordinary becomes that which is already under threat by imagined others whose proximity becomes a crime against person as well as place. The ordinary or normative subject is reproduced as the injured party: the one 'hurt' or even damaged by the 'invasion' of others. (118)

In poetry reviews, the injured party is the Common Reader or Poetry (the latter defined tautologically as *that which the Common Reader desires*). Constructions of antagonistic language-types here reproduce a positional construction of a normative phantasmic reading subject. Although most reviewers hold (at least) undergraduate university degrees, the jargon of Academia corrupts natural language and speech, drives out the Poetic, destroys emotion, is cynical and inhumane. For example, Rob Taylor above can only hear a "mega-syllabic disaster." He reports on the discourse type (the Inhuman jargon), not its content. Weyman Chan, although sympathetic, and a postmodern poet himself, fears the "lofty semiotic nightmare" or paints jargon as something sinister: "[L]anguage languishes as mere encryptions which cast very small shadows indeed against the world's passage" (86). Kathy Shaidle argues that foreign influence, in both nationalist and poetic-essentialist terms, empties poetry of life. School is a poetic bummer:

Sentest "divides his time between Europe and Montreal"; this may explain why these pieces sounded less like poetry than like elevated-yet-empty Eu-ro-style philosophizing. Few of these poems really come alive ... much in-tellectual name-dropping, but not enough heart, soul, or passion. ("Grand Gnostic")

Shaidle, unable to account for her cold response to Sentest's poetry, picks up on a scrap from an author bio to solve her dilemma. Note she reports on the type of language Sentest uses, not its content. "Elevated-yet-emp-ty" is a fair characterisation of what is often intended when "jargon" is used pejoratively. Jargon is just fancy talk. Consequently, Sentest's very name-droppy (of disastrously multi-syllabic names?) writing is like "Eu-ro-style philosophising," not "like poetry." Academic and alien, it has a foreign accent. Like Milton Acorn's warnings about the Bad Mountain, Shaidle warns Canadian Poets to avoid Europe. Here be Eggheads. That word-nerdy stuff they write back there in the old countries is not poetry.

The Tradition

Shaidle's principled irritation at Sentest's Euro-style accent opens the topic of another governing phantasmic trope: the poetic Tradition. Like the Common Reader, the fantasy of Tradition structures poetic desire. At least four positionally complementary, interlocked constructions of Tradition are common, and often appear in the same review. In a single bristling passage, Linda W. Wagner, author of a biography of Sylvia Plath, evokes three of these Traditions:

[1 and 3] Anyone professing to be a 'new' poet today has the usual two routes open to him [sic]. Either he must do what the old masters were doing – organic form, swift image, juxtaposition – and do it better; or he must map a really new course ... [1 and 2] For every claim to innovation, history provides an earlier example of the new method or theme, as antidote.... [2 and 3] The modern reader is hard to please. He demands proof that a newly published poet can excel in one of two alternatives. Does Gregory Orr out-Williams Williams and Ignatow, or does he take us in a new direction? ... [3] Given, this truth: that all readers in the past expected from new poets was a fairly consistent voice, some good poems, and a sense of craft. (89)

The three functions of Tradition here echo those in T.S. Eliot's "Tradition and the Individual Talent." Tradition is:

1 A fantasy trope of Audience. The Tradition is listening. Like the Tolstoy, Lenin and Pushkin of Yevtushenko, the Tradition is an aesthetico-

moral tribunal in aesthetic conscience with a more authoritative presence and detailed figuration than the Common Reader.

2 An implied or named body of texts that constitute the reviewer's textual orthodoxy, which may or may not coincide with the Academic canon. This Top 100 often serves collectively as the model (or object definition) of True Poetry. Authors of these texts often become phantasmic Audience members.

3 Synonymous with Accessible poetry. True Poetry is Accessible. Traditionally, before the aesthetico-moral decadence of the postmodern, Poetry was Accessible. It said what it meant. It was True.

4 Tradition #3 is directly related to Precosky's historically untenable cultural umbrella Tradition, #4: the human, social togetherness, the common meaning, clarity of purpose and belief people had in Simpler Times.

Wagner's aesthetic conscience does not overtly admit to fearing the dilemmas posed by aesthetic change. Instead her conscience claims to be antagonized by frivolous claims to innovation; thus "new" is in scare-quotes. She formulates, as aesthetic duty, the often-seen rule of incremental change, after T.S. Eliot. Contemporary poets' relationship to Tradition, the rule says, is one of obsequious yet competitive conformism. Literary change unfolds like evolution in nature, not as something the poet should, nor actually can, consciously work for. As Stephanie Bolster said above, "true innovation" is rare; other kinds (read: any nonconformity to standards of the Accessible) by implication are unconscionable, spurious claims to newness. Yet the rule of incremental change is challenged by the facts of literary history – including T.S. Eliot's *The Waste Land*. Knowing that famous works by the venerable Old Masters of Traditions #1 and #2 were often unpredictable breakaways, against the incremental rule, the option is generously left open (albeit in the fine-print) for a poet to be a once-in-a-century meteoric paradigm-smashing xenoprovenant Genius, in which case it may occasionally be conscionable for such a poet to chart a "really new course." The only social role this imagines for poetry and poets is to incrementally (over generations) extend the body of texts that constitutes an ultimately self-referential Tradition (Tradition #2). "Antidote" suggests an antidote to silly claims of newness; the antidote is a poison dart to slay such vanity. Note also the appearance of another audience trope – the Modern Reader – constructed positionally against the Reader from Simpler Times. The social role imagined for reading through these readers provides a complement to both the canon-extending duty with which Wagner invests poets, and to the "idle referendum" imperative in current adjudicative reviewing. In Simpler Times, it appears people read poetry mainly to check its pulse; the empty-calorie value referendum has been the imperative not only of reviewers but of readers through all of Tradition.

In the 1970s, the international validity of Canadian culture is an urgent issue for Canadian poetry reviewers, who often evaluate new books of Canadian poetry in competitive comparison with an imagined international, historical canon. Tradition is fantasized in the ways it is above partly as an aspect of the unresolved struggles over the meaning of USAmerican and British literatures for Canadian writers. In this context, adjudicative, mercantile conscience intercedes as an agent of future Tradition, reducing reading to set of chores: judge→ sort→ predict→ judge→ sort→ predict. It is like a mixture of prophecy and dealing with the recycling.

David Carpenter, author of thirteen books, takes a moment aside, in a review of Robert Kroetsch's *Stone Hammer Poems*, to prophesize: "This is not his finest book. He seems destined to be considered by literary historians as primarily a prose-fiction writer" (120). Rather than invest writers and books with Destiny, Stuart Newton adopts the tough love position of the conscientious, unsentimental ruminator. The light of international literary Tradition is the infallible guide of aesthetic conscience.

Unless a double standard is applied to their work, one standard for traditional English and European literature and another standard for Can Lit, then Colombo and Marlatt have not added anything worthwhile to literary tradition. (68)

Newton bravely concludes that all writers, regardless of provenance, must stand equal before the majestic universal law of objective Quality, established by example in the international Tradition. Yet particularized ethics of double (triple, quadruple, quintuple …) standards, which a normative aesthetic conscience rejects as hypocrisy, is exactly what postmodern poetry constructs. Quality can only be contingent to the needs of a local: community, coterie, region, dialect, club, family, group of friends, person next to you, your African grey parrot, yourself, etc. Presuming an international consensus, Newton compiles a Tradition of texts he believes have a unitary global currency as classics. A pertinent question is: what is his source? Nobel Prize lists? Penguin Classics? Harold Bloom's canon? Regardless, Newton's Tradition is a blandly globalized, museological concept of the literary field. To reiterate John Guillory's point: The only place for poetry, as Newton imagines it, is the mausoleum of well-wrought urns, where literatures go to enter an afterlife realm of sheer value after they have risen above the world of power. Any cultural product not marked "Destined for Heritage" is not "worthwhile." Poets like Daphne Marlatt, who pay microscopic attention to the poetic inflections of the local, waste their lives.

Similarly, Charles Lillard, author of seven books of poetry, imagines the Tradition as a stable collection of internationally approved, unproblematic texts, all of which share the all-trumping characteristic of Greatness. Built for transnational cultural export, such texts are not marked by eccentricities of localism, dialect, nor organized by micro-climatic structures of feeling:

Alaska has produced one book…. British Columbia has produced no major poets…. To the southward, Literature is in no better condition. A few novels, and one poet. Robinson Jeffers. Jeffers might have been a major figure, if it had not been for his tragic, essentially warped vision. (144-145)

Greatness here is fantasized as a reliably translatable quality, like a block-buster film that can be subtitled into any language with little semantic loss. Like Wagner above, Lillard has all writers working only for the purpose of adding to the great library of the global Tradition. That "one book" Alaska produced is totally reified: The invisible labour of all other Alaskan writers, like factory workers whose lives buoy the fortune of a single capitalist, contributes silently to raise the value of a single Great book. Postmodern poets' self-publication practices develop through the 1960s and 1970s in direct antagonism to such pseudo-historical, pseudo-global concepts of the literary. Poets adopt their own means of publication and distribution. They form concrete readerships and counter publics that are not the phantasmic Public. Instead of a Penguin Classics paradigm, they push a vision of particularized readerships, and a complex aesthetics of scale. Neither do pseudo-internationalist assertions about her majesty Quality like Lillard's bear out in literary history. Those very qualities that for Lillard mar Greatness – smallness, specificity, eccentric localism, patois, oppositional or alternate readings of literary history, etc. – have gained significant international readerships for Canadian poetry.

Reviewers sometimes take a position near a phantasmic aesthetic overseer from Tradition (i.e., like a mystical Baudelaire, Pushkin, Tolstoy or John Ruskin), from where they perform the moral affect of outrage to associate their own aesthetic identity with that of a celebrity phantasm. This response is most common when the poet him/herself makes a "frivolous" claim of proximity with some canonic phantasm. The reviewer then angrily intercedes as a Common Sense Security Guard protecting a cultural treasure. He/she sides with Tradition against the poet, whom she/he treats as a vandalous interloper. Keep your greasy fingers off the artworks! In this sense, as the actual people writing and publishing poetry, aesthetic conscience fears living poets as the greatest concrete threat to phantasmic Tradition. Actuality threatens the fantasy. Hence the vehemence of reviewers like Bert Almon, author of six books of poetry, who growls that:

[Crystal] Hurdle's verse is undistinguished, the best images coming from Plath's work in a kind of pastiche. Those battered old symbols, Ken and Barbie, are dragged out of the toy box to make a feminist point. Taste aside, Ezra Pound once observed that technique is the test of sincerity, and Ted and Sylvia fails that test. This poet has not earned the right to address Plath as 'Sivvy.' (145)

"Taste aside" – Almon disavows ideology, as he constructs a deeply political antagonism to Hurdle's book. In poetry, feminism can only be a political Barbie doll. The only "sincerity" that counts is objectively, lawfully measurable as Quality, via cold scrutiny of politically neutral technique. The hard realpolitik of Almon's world, meanwhile, is one where a "right" (i.e., food, shelter, healthcare, freedom of speech, addressing Ted Hughes as "Teddie Boy") is morally earned by individual writerly toil, neither given *a priori* nor struggled for collectively. With such distinctions, Almon implicitly separates True Poetry (here: beyond the political) from particularist waste. Books like Hurdle's must be kept from staining museological Greatness with their dirty hands. Hurdle's criminally vicious thefts of Plath's imagery kindle the righteous fire of a lawful outrage. Aesthetic conscience further reassures reviewers like Almon that their indignation is registered (somewhere in a cultural afterlife?) for moral credit. As Phyllis Webb writes: "For [any anthologist] there is a question: have I included a Fredegond Shove and left out a T.S. Eliot?" (150).

Reviewer Zachariah Wells, author of the collections *Unsettled* and *Track & Trace*, takes a bullet for bad poetry, thirty years later, for W.B. Yeats:

There is no dynamism to writing like this, no verbal dexterity, no powerful rhythm, no imagery or metaphor, nothing at all to lift it above the humdrum of quotidian banality the book represents. But ya gotta marvel at the naïve nerve to quote Yeats in the midst of such drek! ("Griffin")

Both reviewers make typical essentialist distinctions between good and bad poetry – distinctions that treat the fact of canonic status as expressive of the books' inherent Quality (and Quality = veracity), rather than status being an outcome of struggles within the poetic field. These examples, like others, elide that Yeats and Plath are not valued equally, nor uniformly, nor universally across the field, and mollify the productive ideological conflicts within their respective works. As Raymond Williams notes in "The Creative Mind," what these reviewers assert as evaluative rigour (the lofty demand that Canadian literature be "competitive" in a transnational, transhistorical literary marketplace) is an "easy but false solution to the problem of quality in art" (29).

Poetry

From the normative sweep of the reviews above, I infer that the tempo-
rality of this phantasmic Tradition is unconnected to the uneven, dif-
ferentiated temporalities of daily life, or to the actual social struggles of
history. The Tradition is quasi-mythological; its temporality is like what
Mikhail Bakhtin calls indefinite, mythic *"adventure time*, highly intensi-
fied but undifferentiated … [without] natural, everyday cyclicity" (90-1
my emphasis), or the long, frozen moment of stilled time inside a mu-
seum. T.S. Eliot articulates that temporality in "Tradition and the Indi-
vidual Talent." He writes that

*the historical sense compels a man to write not merely with his own gen-
eration in his bones, but with a feeling that the whole life of the literature
of Europe from Homer and within it the whole of the literature of his own
country has a simultaneous existence and composes a simultaneous order.
This historical sense, which is a sense of the timeless and the temporal to-
gether, is what makes a writer traditional…. The existing monuments form
an ideal order among themselves, which is modified by the introduction of
the new (the really new) work of art among them.* (499)

This super-synchronic temporality (i.e., all of literature as a single mo-
ment) becomes in fantasy not only the time of Tradition, but of a fan-
tastical Poetry. And so Poetry itself, as an unquotidian but Accessible,
magical place to go, as well as the ideal object of desire, is one of the
phantasmic tropes of aesthetic conscience.

As Jameson argues in "The Barrier of Time," the "ideological illusion" of Poetry as supersynchronic pushes poetry into the temporal space of myth.

The more successful the historiographic construction [of the synchronic] – the conviction that everything is of a piece, that the relations between existences and facts are much stronger than their possible relationship to what is no longer and what is not yet, that actuality is a seamless web and the past (or tradition) a mere intellectual construct in the present – the stronger this case is made intellectually, the more inevitable is our entry into a Parmenidean realm in which some eternal system reigns around us like a noon beyond time only faintly perfumed with the odour of heated plangs and informed by the echo of cicadas and the distant and incomprehensible memory of death ... the more airtight the synchronic system laid in place all around us, the more surely history itself evaporates in the process, and along with it any possibility of political agency or collective anti-systemic praxis. (89)

The Tradition as timeless myth, poetry as phantasmic Poetry, depoliticizes actual poetry by removing it from the social sites of its production and reception, yanks it out of concrete history. The marks of concrete struggle in the work are obscured, suppressed or rendered illegible.

Poetry as a phantasm operates in at least two competing temporalities: in the Parmenidean realm or mythological past of Tradition, and in a mythological future of Destiny, as a fantasy in the vulgar sense of "wish-fulfilment." Future Tradition. Reviewers dream of Poetry, poets aspire to Poetry, while few in the history of poetics have been certain that (the strawberry cake of) poetic fantasy substantially exists. Like an hallucination, Poetry hovers in view, as ungraspable as Macbeth's dagger. Poetry, as phantasm, is an absent ideal, a present but uncertain phenomenon in/of the Parmenidean realm of Eliot's ideal order. (Note that Tradition and Poetry as phantasm often fold into one another.) Poetry as phantasm shifts between being a mythical place to go, and an object of pure, distilled value-as-value. (Perhaps Poetry is the museum, and the Poem is the gemstone?) In this schema, a complementary structural tension holds between the everyday as compositional, representational field (the subject matter and lexical content that constitutes Accessbility) and the universal (or infinite) towards which the Common Reader is supposed to be jolted through re-encounter with these particularities in Accessible poetry. All synecdoche all the time – dirty dirt is always transmuted into mythical Earth.

In "The Creative Mind," Raymond Williams identifies this very tension of poetry as an absent ideal. Although Williams quotes from Percy Shelley's "Defense of Poetry," certain passages he overlooks seem to demonstrate better the tensions that Shelley marks. As for many reviewers now, quotidian detail is always a synecdochal sign of mythical time:

Poets ... were called in the earlier epochs of the world legislators or prophets: a poet essentially comprises and unites both these characters. For he [sic] not only beholds intensely the present as it is, and discovers those laws according to which present things ought to be ordered, but he beholds the future in the present, and his thoughts are the germs of the flower and the fruit of latest time.... A Poet participates in the eternal, the infinite, and the one; as far as relates to his conceptions, time and place and number are not. (341-342)

Poetry indeed here participates in and observes the everyday only to the extent that it "withdraws life's dark veil from before the scene of things ... [and] purges from our inward sight the film of familiarity which obscures from us the wonder of our being" (qtd. in Williams 10). Modernism largely retains this fantasy of Poetry, and hands it down to permamodern Canadian poetry reviewers. As Liliane Welch, author of over twenty-one collections of poetry, writes in a review of books by Hédi Bouraoui and Harry Thurston: "the violence of nature, the pressure of

173

history are [sic] sung within the context of a form which guarantees an ultimate harmony, and which preserves as it transcends" (112).

The sometimes mysteriously and unevenly archaic, thesaurus-dependent style of Canadian poetry reviews is somewhat illuminated in this context. Why many reviewers choose phrases such as "volume of verse" instead of "book of poetry," (or "latest effort," "deft lyricism," "polished in craft," "dutifully ostentatious," "weighty tome," "standard of excellence," "passionate fervour"; words like "one," "lamentable," "poster-ity," "accolade," "laudatory," "laureate," "deem," etc.) has been a puzzle throughout my research. The phony British accent in passages like the following, from the same Greg Gatenby review quoted above, sounds lived, yet somewhere far from the living room:

Canada's senior anthologist [A.J. M. Smith] is also ... a very highly re-spected poet in some quarters, although kudos for his poetry have never been as overwhelming as they have been for other versifiers.... I also sus-pect though that the reading of Smith's poetry, like Guinness, is an acquired taste, and like that noble brew may be deemed less than essential by other-wise regular imbibers of literature. (119)

This colonial-anachronistic voice now appears to me to be a constitutive part of the construction of Poetry as a phantasmic, mythical place and ideal, as fetishised value-object, and as part of the construction of Tradi-tion as phantasmic governor of aesthetic conscience. Poetry is a place visited by many reviewers as if by a Victorian time machine of (discur-sive) brass, ebony, ivory and quartz.

One of the Few Genuine Remaining Hardware Stores:
The Discourse of Craft

If it feels malign, as it might, that I am about to critique the discourse of craft, the strength of that feeling indexes the strength of craft's hegemony. Both inside and outside the restricted linguistic economy of the book review, poetry is spontaneously associated with a notion of craft, and conceived through its discourse. Books about poetry marketed for the Common Reader constantly reinforce the association. Craft, in these circumstances, is sometimes treated as a gateway concept, or as a ground-level entry concept that will help the Subject Supposed to Be Curious but Not Know Very Much think about poetry.

Titles of populist books on poetry often privilege craft: *The Craft of Poetry: Structure & Sound* (2011); *A Poet's Craft: A Comprehensive Guide to Making and Sharing Your Poetry* (2011); *Next Word, Better Word: The Craft of Writing Poetry* (2011); *The Art and Craft of Poetry: Twenty Exercises Toward Mastery* (2009); *Writing Poetry from the Inside Out: Finding Your Voice Through the Craft of Poetry* (2007); *Real Sofistikashun: Essays On Poetry And Craft* (2006); *The Verse Book Of Interviews: 27 Poets On Language, Craft & Culture* (2005); *The Eye of the Poet: Six Views of the Art and Craft of Poetry* (2001); *The Craft of Writing Poetry* (2000); *Poet's Notebook: Inspiration, Techniques, and Advice on Craft* (2000). But the anachronistic equation POETRY IS CRAFT, while poetry continues to pluralize in ways that re-define the meanings of writerly skill, is rarely left at the beginner's gate: it remains fundamental to informed poet-reviewers' discourse on poetry.

The equation POETRY IS CRAFT is what cognitive scientist George

Lakoff calls a "metaphoric theme" or "root analogy" (qtd. in Goatly 25). In his Marxian applications of Lakoff's theories in "Ideology and Metaphor," Goatly provides a few commonsense examples of such themes: POWER IS HIGH; SEX IS VIOLENCE; TIME IS MOVEMENT; TIME IS MONEY; QUALITY IS MONEY/WEALTH. In cognitive linguistic science, theories of latent metaphor in language tend to be based on a contrast of "living" (consciously deployed) against "dead" (unconscious, embedded) metaphors. The premise at work – which productively recalls Viktor Shlovsky's concept of the poetic device as one of "enstrangement [sic]" (11) – is that a metaphor "dies" in language through habituation, after which it continues to silently shape thought and behaviour. A metaphor begins its downward career as a brilliant convergence of two seemingly disparate things, gradually losing its power of enstrangement as it becomes embedded in everyday idiom. Yet, in their study "Metaphors, Idiom and Ideology," Michael Billig and Katie MacMillan argue that the Lakoffian model "is too simple to account for the complex, rhetorical processes by which a metaphor might pass from a striking, novel comparison into an unthinking idiom" (460). In their corrective extension of Lakoff's framework, theorizing how metaphor pragmatically passes into idiom (or ideolect), and thereby becomes constitutive of ideology, they elaborate: "There is another way that idiom can contribute to ideology. The metaphorical vehicle may not simply wear down, or run over, the topic. But the topic can ground the vehicle … the metaphorical idiom can also dull literal meaning to the point of ideological concealment" (478).

The passage from idiom to full-blown ideolect is achieved in the self-interpellative processes of pragmatic use: ritual or generic iterative repetition, and conscientious deliberation. These processes, however, do not merely "wear down" or "kill" metaphors: they root them more firmly in linguistic practice, where they become part of the dynamic ground of ideation, affect and identity. As ground, the metaphors occupy a place between the states of life and death, both unconsciously habitual in use and actively extended in new re-iterations and elaborations. In the reproduction of any ideolect, a dynamic complementary relationship holds between "unthinking" use of a root metaphor, wherein, as Billig and MacMillan write, they are used "literally rather than in a consciously metaphorical way" (463), and the deliberate, conscious extension of its lexicon.

My project in this chapter therefore starts as a hybrid between fantasy/ideology critique, and a cognitive linguistics approach to embedded metaphor. I collect "clusters of common metaphors" (Billig and MacMillan 462) out of commonplace crafts discourse and subject them to critical analysis. (And again, it seems important to reiterate, in analysing specific reviews I rarely make claims about a reviewer's other writings, and absolutely never intend anything like personal or ad-hominem attacks on individuals. This is a book about texts, not persons.) In my analysis, rather than "hypothesize inner cognitive states" (ibid.), I take a somewhat more pragmatic discourse-analytical turn to "examine particular uses of metaphors and, by paying attention to the contexts of utterance, note what the users of such metaphors are doing rhetorically and pragmatically" (ibid.), whilst unpacking ideological assumptions and implications. What concerns a critique such as this is the congress of the living and the dead in discourse, how the metaphors in crafts discourse, in every instantiation, are given the "kiss of life and then left to die in a different graveyard" (Billig and MacMillan 477).

Consider some common crafts terms recurrent in poetry reviews: accurate, apprentice, balance, carve, clear, concise, consistent, control, craft, fine, finish, forge, form, grind, hone, integrity, job, mastery, material, wrought, precise, purpose, polish, refine, sharp, shine, skill, strength, sturdy, task, technique, toil, trade, tune, work. Although the job-identity of the phantasmic Poet is predominantly masculine, "hard craft" and "handicraft" sometimes intersect. Passages of poetry are "finely worked," poems are "well-woven," they are "stylishly constructed," or "tightly constructed" or "finely fashioned." Poets can "forge a way to write," material

elements are "worked into" a poem, the trick is "maintaining balance."
Weyman Chan's review of *Year Zero*, quoted above, begins in a splendid
flourish of mixed metaphors, drawn from a crafts lexicon:

So much depends on darkness and light, catalysts of the human imagina-
tion. Brian Henderson's latest offering in that richly varied poetic career of
his, spins untold gems of wisdom out of a thick brocade of birds and but-
terflies, eclipses and mystical states of mind. He coins it 'a kind of turning
and/recalling embodiment,' this typography of language he gives us. (83)

Crafts discourse often serves as the fundament of value constructions
in poetry reviews, heavily relied on consciously and unconsciously – at
once dead and alive. As Billig and McMillan paraphrase Lakoff: "One
might say that the living metaphor starts dying once it begins to live
within language" (461). Crafts discourse is naturalised as the correct
(obvious, unthinking) way to write about the work of writing poetry.
That POETRY IS CRAFT is common sense. Its already large, pervasive
lexicon is also deliberately extended by many reviewers. In conscientious
practice, between ideological death and ideational life, crafts discourse
finally becomes so bound up with the sensual, affective experiences of
poetry that it seems untheorizable. An ideolect is, non-paradoxically, the
most dead (uncritical) type of language, and the most insidiously (cre-
atively) alive. When the habituation becomes deep enough, metaphori-
cal terms can come to appear self-evident, literal descriptors of some-
thing poetry substantially is.

Metaphors We Craft By

My critique of crafts discourse in the reviewer's ideolect is guided by three related lines of concern:

1 The ambivalence in reviews about issues of labour/work, particularly insofar as forms of labour function as positional markers of identity and class, and insofar as the aesthetic conscience of Canadian poetry reviewers frequently assesses poetic value as accumulated relative to writerly labour expended. Reviewers find a false solution to the problem of quality in art through a kind of poet's labour theory of value.[14]

2 The equally deep ambivalence about class positions as such, and how they intersect with or produce positions in the poetic field. Reviewers reveal shifty, unstable notions and assumptions about the class positions of poets and readers, and, no less, a nervous uncertainty about which class interests are served by the culture of poetry.

3 The tendency, as outlined above, to describe poetry and language in crafts terms that function to substantiate both for ideology. A rigidly conscientious – as opposed to rigorous – adjudicative project seems to require an object more substantial than the liquid hologram strawberry cake of poetry. Any critical discourse on poetry confronts the sore problem of poetry's inadequate substantiality – which is the same

---

14 By contrast, Romantic notions of inspiration, of the poetic *shazam!*, only persist in brackets, as quasi-supernatural, once in a lifetime events. Genius is 5% inspiration, 95% perspiration, as Einstein said – reviewers assent.

problem that confronts any linguist – and finds an ideological balm in metaphor.

As language, poetry always lacks features it might share with other phenomena that would ground a connecting analogy. Billig and Mac-Millan draw from Aristotle "the example of old age as 'a dried stalk'" (460). This analogy is co-grounded by concrete features the aged person and the stalk share: dryness and baldness. "The notion of dryness and losing flowers is thus transferred from the stalk to the notion of age" (ibid.). In reality, poetry does not share any such common feature with the items of crafts discourse. Making a poem is in no sense concretely like, say, the blacksmithery suggested in the commonplace crafts analogy "wordsmith." What features do language and poetry share with other phenomena that might stably ground analogies? Only, perhaps, mutability. This is why the Russian philosopher of language Mikhail Bakhtin returns repeatedly, even obsessively, to analogies between language and water – reported speech in Charles Dickens's prose, Bakhtin writes, is: "washed by heteroglot waves from all sides" (309). As language, and as a time-based medium that cannot be frozen, poetry never adequately confirms the qualities of substantiality or objecthood posited for it in crafts discourse. A false, but commanded, solution of adjudicative reviewers is often an elaborate fantasy empiricism, metaphorically rooted in crafts discourse.

Various related questions compel the aesthetic reasoning performed in poetry reviews: What is a poem? What type of work is the writing of poetry? Is it aesthetico-morally safe to identify with the poet under review? Is it possible to be certain about value? What are the limits of poetry's facticity? How much privilege does this poet command? How does privilege affect poetry? What is poetry's position in the hierarchy of cultural forms? On what bases can one make claims for poetry's cultural importance? Who are poetry's antagonists? How is poetry best defended from its antagonists? Such questions emerge from structural tensions within the poetic field, and their irresolution is an impetus in both poetic practice and in reviewing practice. To take up an argument made by Stuart Hall in "The Problem of Ideology: Marxism Without Guarantees," ideolect: "provides the repertoire of categories which will be used, in thought" (44). Ideolect becomes, in reiterative practice, the material medium of a literary ideology. Ideology, however, is not a closed circuit, nor is ideolect an absolute determiner. As Hall asserts: "The paradigm of perfectly closed, perfectly predictable, systems of thought is religion or astrology, not science" (45). Despite the powerful centripetal pull of aesthetic conscience, even in the most strictly adjudicative reviewing project multiple discursive frames overlap, inevitably contradicting each other in self-subverting ways – the always present condition of ideological leakage, excess and overflow. In this way Michael Davidson writes of the "proliferation of discursive frames, 'social heteroglossia,' and their interaction, 'dialogization'. The active interchange among these levels ... [which] reflect a similar dialogue among social codes (ideologemes) occurring in the world at large" (144).

Reviewers' local answers to any of the implicit or explicit orienting questions thus become flashpoint sites in the positions struggles of the poetic field. Internal to the cultural field, these struggles simultaneously parallel, reflect, reproduce, or even parody, struggles in the broader social field. As with the metamorphosing phantasms of the Common Reader, although reviewers do not answer these questions with an immovable formula, crafts discourse provides the reviewer's ideolect the categories in which the answers are conceived. As Gramsci writes, these categories "become matrices in which thought takes shape out of flux" (373). The determining effects of the ideolect require, as Stuart Hall extends Gramsci's argument:

[u]nderstanding 'determinacy' in terms of setting of limits, the establishment of parameters, the defining of the space of operations, the concrete conditions of existence, the 'givenness' of social practices, rather than in terms of the absolute predictability of particular outcomes. (45)

In Some Legendary Place

Detailed personifications of the Common Reader often force reviewers' class biases into view. Very often the figuration of the Common Reader is dependent on projections of the reviewer's own class assumptions, or on the desire for a cultural class ascendancy that pervades Canadian literary culture. The class of the Common Reader may be the reviewer's class (e.g., "average middle class"). Elsewhere it might be the class into which the reviewer wants poetry (and poets) to be incorporated ("retired engineer"). In the crafts discourse of poetry reviews, the question of class position often manifests as a similarly interrogative comparison of the phantasmic ideal Poet with the author actually under review. Aesthetic conscience asks: What is the morally appropriate class position of the poet? Answers to this question are often constructed indirectly, through the conceptualisation of poetry as a form of work. As reflections of realities beyond than the cultural field, forms of work are taken as a direct index of class position. A *Marquis* does a certain type of work, a *sans-papiers* does another. So answers to the underlying question – what is the poet's labour? – assert answers to broader questions of cultural and class positioning that organise the poetic field. Is the phantasmic Poet a skilled labourer, a member of a cultural bourgeoisie, of a clerical-managerial class, or part of a quasi-religious, quasi-spiritual autonomous elite? As sociologist John Myles summarizes Bourdieu's linguistics, language practice is

just another form of more general social practices of [class] distinction ...

the 'language market' … should itself be seen as having been structured by past struggles over the value of its different areas of practice.… Thus the character of a class's trajectory depends on how a class fares in its struggles over value in the linguistic field. (883-5)

Anxious ambivalence about class positions is a determining aspect of the struggles to define and articulate the Canadian poetic field, symptomatic, among other things, of poetry's uncertain position in the hierarchy of cultural forms. "Poetry" survives broadly as an honorific category – as when a compliment is paid: "Oh, how poetic!" – while the practice is culturally marginal. Poetry is a nest of cultural contradictions, symbolically superdeluxe but a financial good-for-nothing. What Hal Foster calls the "lobotomy" of the cultural "brow system" (6) has made poetry's position on the brow registry even more uncertain. The irritant question: Is poetry highbrow, middlebrow, lowbrow or nobrow? For many Canadian reviewers, poetry's long afterlife as an honorific category, and thus its symbolic cultural value, depends on its association with highbrow cultural values (as Raymond Williams noted in "The Creative Imagination"), while the poet's concrete class position may be indeterminate or unambiguously low. In the latter case, if the poet's initial class position is lowly, an innocence is purchased for poetry that can make the most cravenly hierarchical reviewing practices conscionable.

In *Writing Degree Zero*, Roland Barthes traces the historical origins of these positional anxieties, and suggests how they changed dominant cultural concepts of writing as a practice and as a form of work. Within the bourgeois public sphere – which Barthes characterises as an empiricist, economist culture of trade and bureaucracy – around 1850 literature "begins to face a problem of self-justification" (62). In Barthes' view, literature re-secures its cultural place not by rejection of the given terms, which was the radical move that many modernist, postmodern and otherwise politicized poets would eventually make. Instead poets totally incorporate these terms into the phantasmic, linguistic apparatus of literary culture and its aesthetic conscience. As the aesthetic conscience of literary culture is reshaped around an economist cultural logic, the class status of the writer, and the status of writing as a form of labour, become linchpin issues in positions struggles.

Although writing about the 19th century France, the ideolect Barthes sketches remains the dominant in Canadian poetry reviewing today:

There begins now to grow up an image of the writer as a craftsman who shuts himself [sic] away in some legendary place, like a workman operating at home and who roughs out, cuts, polishes, and sets his form exactly as a jeweller extracts art from his material, devoting to his work regular hours of solitary effort.... Writing is now to be saved not by virtue of what it exists for, but what it has cost. Labour replaces genius as a value, so to speak; there is a kind of ostentation in claiming to labour long and lovingly over the form of one's work. There even arises, sometimes, a preciosity of conciseness (for laboring at one's material usually means reducing it). (Writing 63)

This "image of the writer" is another phantasmic figure in aesthetic conscience, with the poet virtuously crafting quality goods for that other phantasm: the Common Reader. A conception of the poet as skilled worker is a key premise in Canadian poetry reviews. The "job of the poet" is a demanding, rewarding (symbolically, spiritually, culturally, personally, not financially), conscionable if carried out with diligence and virtuous aesthetic intent.[15] The "legendary place" Barthes mentions is normally the site of the craftsman's toil (the workshop or studio or office), or of the reward for such labour (permanent vacation in "Canada's Parnassus," perhaps, or a long poetic Sabbath in the modest, taste-

---

15 Poetry, as Bourdieu writes: "proves its authenticity by the fact that it secures no remuneration.... [it] finds its criterion of authenticity in disinterestedness" (*Rules* 216).

fully furnished livingroom of the retired engineer). And here, both on grounds of work and exchange, language is increasingly described as if it has a substantiality which the craftsman can bend to his/her mastery, to produce the hardened cultural artifact or the shiny affective moment-producing machine of the poem. In aesthetic conscience, the craftsman also often occupies an accommodating intermediate class position: Well-paid (the elite of the imaginary working class), skilled (educated *and* practical), producer of luxury goods (specialized commerce dependent on the demands of an imaginary upper class, or highbrow caste). Low enough for moral innocence, but high enough to serve the highbrow, the POET AS CRAFTSMAN is not only a node of authenticist resistance to the postmodern condition of inauthenticity, he [sic] provides a morally opportune class compromise within that condition.

A Genuine Hardware Store

In his review of a book of selected poems by prolific Maritime poet and publisher Fred Cogswell, J.K. Snyder, an English professor retired from St. Mary's University, imagines the scene of Cogswell's poetry in crafty terms:

The poetry is not always beautiful, nor often even very handsome, but there is a solidity of execution which grows on the reader and an unpretentious seriousness that commands respect. The pleasure one gets from this book is quite like that one has in finding one of the few remaining genuine hardware stores: a quiet, darkish place, with a settled sense of work and notion of order that honours the idea of craft, knowing as it does, that all serious craft is in the service of the beautiful, and, as far as we can make it, the true. (156)

"Pleasure" here already marks the social territory of poetry as narrow, it orients poetry away from other possible cultural politics. By the time the word *craft* actually appears, that metaphor and its ramifications have already been elaborated in multiple ways, particularly through the extended analogy of the hardware store, as the site of substance, work, craft and commerce. The term "genuine" invokes craft discourse's authenticist connotations. "One of the few" evokes the rare, legendary place of toil where the craftsman labours, unsentimentally driven by a "settled sense of work," without which poetry cannot accrue value. The craftsman here, with his "notion of order," of rational artistic form, produces poetry not out of a sense of love, play, jouissance, curiosity or political passion, but out of sober, conscientious aesthetic duty. Such poetry operates as a conservative social force, not as a critical social force. The reviewer's pleasure is that of "respect" – a moral affect here connected to the virtue accrued through labour – for "solidity of execution." Indeed, Cogswell's poetry appears to be valuable mainly for how it makes poetry seem substantial, solid. As Michael Davidson writes: "the reader [here] may only witness, in a passive sense, the author's testimony" (143).

The fantasy of the endangered hardware store positions poetry in a cultural past. It heroises the poet as part of a vanishing "way of life," or disappearing social relations. Permamodern poetry is a categorical antagonist to postmodern poetries. Snyder echoes Jameson's valuation of modernist depth (e.g., Van Gogh) against postmodern vacuity (e.g., Warhol), marking an ideological distance from postmodernity: The phantasmic past of Simpler Times is where all things genuine reside, and the present is a time of truthless inauthenticity. Nostalgic reviewing such as this often writes its way willy-nilly into neo-conservative values, however "liberal" or "left" or even anarchist (e.g., George Woodcock) its departure points. Because Snyder leaves unstated his definition of the feminine "beautiful," against the masculine "handsome," his implicit definitions (pleasure, sobriety, seriousness, work, order, authenticity, masculinity) fill the lacuna of the unsaid. The hesitant clause, "as far as we can see it," seals this notion of the beautiful into the sarcophagus of an inadvertent pun: poetic-emotional "truth," and the carpenter's "true."

As Jürgen Habermas argues in "Modernity – An Unfinished Project," reviewers' ambivalent relationship with postmodern poetry can also be read in light of modernity's (and capitalism's) grossly unfulfilled promises, as well as in terms of position-takings in the poetic field. Even while the superficial pluralization of cultural forms and technological means continue to accelerate, an observer can lament that "the project of modernity has not yet been fulfilled" (12). Neoliberal capitalism keeps on promising, and keeps on deferring. In Habermas' words "the disillusionment with the very failures of those programs [of modernization, education, science and objectivity] that called for a negation of art and philosophy has come to serve as a pretence for conservative positions" (13-14). David Solway's retired engineer and Snyder's hardware store are evidence that, as Jürgen Habermas argues, for many writers:

These experiments [of modernism and postmodernism] have served to bring back to life, and to illuminate all the more glaringly, exactly those structures of art which they were meant to dissolve. They gave a new legitimacy, as ends in themselves, to appearance as the medium of fiction, to the transcendence of the artwork over society, to the concentrated and planned character of artistic production as well as the special cognitive status of judgements of taste. (11)

As to the masculinism of crafts discourse, the associations of the hardware store with masculine work activity remains culturally strong. The dominant fantasy of the Poet as a craftsman tends to conceive poetry as a masculine-gendered form of work. This positioning, arising in relation to the fantasy empiricism, reflects the search for a solid (objective, lawful) ground on which to evaluate poetry. Patriarchal ideology associates the masculine with qualities affectively harmonious with empirical certainty: muscular strength, solidity and with economic (rather than affective or domestic) productivity. A poet-craftsman's work is therefore more often conceived through masculine-gendered tropes like: carpentry, masonry, gem cutting. These rather than: knitting, lace-making, sewing. The latter, feminine craft – often gendered as "handicraft" – are used to diminish poetry as inauthentic (feminine, effeminate, effete) work.

The poet of Snyder's hardware store, subtly figured as a carpenter, is therefore more likely to evoke Milton Acorn than Margaret Avison, Ken Babstock than Kate Braid. Snyder has a moment of self-reflection about this acute gender slant, then swiftly mops up the ideological spill: "I suppose it is man's poetry, but one of those rare men strong enough to love and to absorb the hurt in loving" (156). He implicitly contrasts the postmodern male with an authentic modern male; the former is effete, weak, unserious, feminized. Beyond the ideologically overdetermined gender of the phantasmic carpenter, in the rest of the review the extensions of POETRY IS CRAFT into descriptive language are equally masculinist. Cogswell's poetry shows "solidity of execution;" "commands respect;" is "strong;" shows that he has "mastered" his material and tends to be "bigger and better" than most. The last of the Genuine Hardware Stores, legendary place, is the site of such manly poetry, of such narrow ideology.

Not as Funny as Seinfeld

The issues at stake are not so much of the correct representations of poetry, as the drastic limits crafts discourse forces on the imagination of poetry's means, use and social consequence. To reiterate: Ideology is produced, and reproduced, in iterative material processes of social ritual and conscience. In his notes towards a theory of ideology, Althusser famously adapted Pascal's insight that, rather than express belief, religious rituals produce belief. "Kneel down, move your lips in prayer, and you will believe" (168). As Althusser's critics have retorted, in itself this is insufficient: Ritual must both express belief and produce belief. Given, but Althusser still accentuates the process correctly: ritual is far more *productive* of belief than it is *expressive* of belief. Language use is a social ritual that can express belief. Moreso, language use produces the beliefs it appears to express. In the restricted linguistic economy of a poetry reviewer's evaluative ideolect, the belief produced is a commensurate mode of poetic value. As Bourdieu writes in *The Rules of Art*, these values take on an objective, natural character:

The 'subjective' dispositions which are at the source of value have, as products of a historical process of institution, the objectivity of something established in a collective order which transcends consciousness and individual wills…. [T]he libido at its root presents all the appearances of nature … to minds – that is, habitus – fashioned by its structures. (172-3)

And, as reviewers above have shown, belief in a text's value is often inseparable from the belief that it is poetry. With some reviewers, non-contingent quality becomes the socially amputated, circular definition of poetry as such. Likewise, POETRY IS CRAFT, the reproduction of the discourse of craft, produces values for apparently commensurate forms, modes and practices of poetry. The restricted social roles for poetry it imagines engage primarily an economist paradigm of luxury trade.

Reviewers struggle with the ideolect, because it does not – cannot – recuperate all the complexities of reader response, because it is grossly inadequate to all poetry of any type. Yet this ideolect, driven by the imperative of judgement, constitutes the generic laws of the review, to the extent that actual, complex, digressive responses have to be simplified into this ideolect as a matter of aesthetic conscience. Complexity is obscured, or redacted, in the fulfilment of aesthetic juror's duty to an audience of phantasmic tropes, through the discourse of craft. Crafts discourse in particular produces a fantasy empiricism that must read the literary values it produces as not only non-contingent, but as substantially inherent in the poem. To achieve an ideology of non-contingent values, words are gradually, meticulously removed from the pragmatic contingencies of discourse.

What can it mean to praise or denigrate for their craftsmanship different poets whose aesthetic imperatives, and entire poetics, are contradictory or actively antagonistic with each other? d.h. sullivan, author of the collection *Wind, Sun, Stone and Ice*, writes appreciatively of Lionel Kearns:

Next to all this hard-nosed work poetry, Lionel Kearns' reflective approach to things is soft, personal, almost romantic at times. Some of the old Kearns' standards have been reprinted here, including such masterpieces as 'The Birth of God' and 'Transport', both of which show his superb awareness of language and craft. (134)

As does rob mclennan in his review of Barry MacKinnon above, when faced with Kearns' work, rather than try to work out new terms of value, or reach for a different colour of ideolectical ink, sullivan attempts to construct value for Kearns' book in the terms of the dominant ideolect. He argues that Kearns' visual poetry is stuff of quality in a known sense, rather than demonstrate how such writing necessarily shifts definitions of quality to contribute to a new mode of value. In his sincere desire to make cultural room for Kearns's poetry, sullivan's strategy is, unfortunately, to argue for the acceptance of these poems as objects of sublime craftsmanship – as masterpieces. Note also sullivan's shifts of ethos. As per capitalist redactions of actual daily work conditions from the cultural imaginary, Kearn's "hard nosed" work poetry is not masterpieceful, while his "almost romantic" concrete work might just be.

To assume equality where none exists is oppression. As Anatole France famously writes: "The law, in its majestic equality, forbids the rich and the poor alike to sleep under bridges, to beg in the streets, and to steal bread." No single value system, such as the one that emerges with crafts discourse, can "objectively" account for divergent aesthetic imperatives, particularly when those poetics are defined through a process of antagonistic differentiation against dominant poetics. Crafts discourse cannot account for postmodern poetries. So to submit Kearns' nonconformist poetry to the discourse of craft (and to the reifying trope of the masterpiece), especially as praise, is to curtail whatever contribution Kearns' work might make to a development of alternate poetic values. It recuperates otherwise transformative work, and potentially nulls its productive effects in the poetic field.

Twenty-four years later, Neil Querengesser, a professor of English at Concordia University College of Alberta, writes that poet Karen Shenfeld has:

remarkable poetic gifts and has clearly worked hard at perfecting her craft. She attends to the finer details of diction, patterns of sound and image, and subtle rhythms and phrasing that result in many polished poetic gems. (129–131)

A phrase such as "her craft" can sometimes indicate that the reviewer critically extends the discourse of craft by consciously pluralizing its definition, in concession that different poetics obey different crafty imperatives. sullivan may have had a particularised notion of craft in mind when he reviewed Kearns' book for example – his concept of the "masterpiece" might be poetically local. If so, by not indicating the specificity of his terms he necessarily subjects Kearns' work to adjudication by dominant, commonsense poetic values. Querengesser, in the sentence that follows, lists the universal set of attentions and skills that constitute expertise in poetry: by "her craft," he indeed means The Craft. These features retroactively define what "poetic" is. Poetry is an assemblage of those features that provide the best guarantee of poetic objecthood an adjudicative reviewer can hope for. To see these poetic qualities assembled in the same text is to see poetry. Shendle, he writes, has "clearly worked hard" because all the features appear present. Yet as critics like Stanley Fish (in "How to Recognize a Poem When You See One" and "How Ordinary is Ordinary Language?") and poets of transcription like Kenneth Goldsmith demonstrate, all putatively "poetic" qualities are discoverable in the most everyday language. In Fish's terms, poetic qualities are not something in the poem, poetic qualities are products of a reading practice. Poetry is a way of paying attention. In Fish's formulation:

In other words, acts of recognition, rather than being triggered by formal characteristics, are [the] source [of poetic qualities]. It is not that the presence of poetic qualities compels a certain kind of attention but that the paying of a certain kind of attention results in the emergence of poetic qualities. ("How to Recognize" 326)

So Querengesser, impelled to validate the hard work of craft, reads to discover licit poetic qualities, specifically those that can be taken for signs of hard work. Shendle's "poetic gifts," her talent, is as much in the poetry's raw material as language is. Here, talent is the actual base matter upon which the craftsman [sic] works with hammers, chisels and sandpaper.

As different figuring analogies connote different poetics, the resultant "gems" of poetry can only function socially in prescribed ways. If the poem is a hand grenade, for example, it has a different social role (or use) than an urn. If the poem is a discursive situation, it cannot also be an artisanal cheese. In this line of analysis, "gem" (a value term that comes up often in poetry reviews) figures pure value – value for value's sake. A gem's social utility is that it stores value *as* value. Reviewers argue, directly or indirectly, that a reader's principal role is to hold a petty value referendum (is it good or is it bad?), either to passively reject or passively admire the static, scintillating value object.

A central aspect of the project of postmodern poetry is to widen the parameters of poetry's use-value, a collective project to continually reimagine what poetry's social role might be. To postmodern poets, this is to make poetry a critical art practice rather than a crafts practice. Crafts discourse only pertains if its object is designed to produce repeatable effects or functions. In poetry, these would be functions or effects far more specific than even the historical avant-garde's call for the ever new, or Victor Shklovsky's call for devices of "enstrangement [sic]" (11). Tables, leather boots, artisanal beer, cupboards, well-wrought ashtrays – these crafted objects perform and embody utilitarian value by a repeatable functionality that reads, reflexively, as the materialisation of a virtuous work ethic. The thing works well = the craftsman has done his [sic] job. The gemstone, as analogy, brings these two strands together. The perfect object of value-as-value emerges from a lot of no-nonsense toil. In addition, a gem has high value in the legitimate monetary economy. In literature, the only modes that might be usefully described in utilitarian terms of craft are strictly generic: romance novels, westerns, mysteries. In such specialised genres, a special form of functionality supersedes (for the most part) symbolic value. As reviewers often say: "It does what it does well." "It is a perfect genre exercise," reviewers say. A craftsperson,

197

so to speak, becomes an expert artisan, a skilled worker, when he/she can produce a more or less identical object or effect each time.

In this way, crafts discourse – as any ideolect would – creates poetic value for certain types of poems, those which perform Poem as a fantasy and as a value, and as a form of genre literature. Versus the exploratory curiosity in postmodern poetries, POETRY IS CRAFT creates comparatively specific, non-contingent, quality imperatives which achieve material social force through reiteration in reviews. Certain types of poets and their corresponding positions in the cultural field have guaranteed cultural capital – a vicious cycle of "success," circular, self-sufficient. Poets are rudely shifted out of the impractical arts, as it were, into the trades, whether by a reviewer like Carmine Starnino (who published an essay called: "Canadian Poets Learn Your Trade") or in Sheldon Currie's mixed appreciation of David W. McFadden: "Nevertheless there are some excellent poems in this book and anyone who can write an excellent poem can write more excellent poems" (111). The Excellent Poem becomes a literary genre the poet learns to reliably produce. Again, poetry that contests these terminological boundaries (that might pose a deep challenge to a crafts based construction of value) is rendered difficult, inaccessible or illegible. In this mode of value, such poetry cannot accrue value. Yet in postmodern poetry, as Charles Altieri argues, the situational contingency of value becomes a core compositional premise: "Value must be rediscovered, not recreated, and this is the challenge accepted by postmodern poetry" (617). In contrast, reviewer Alex Good (unusually, a prolific reviewer of poetry without a book of his own) offers the dominant generic formula of Canadian poetry as a sarcastic aside, in a review of *Americana* by John Updike: middlebrow, accessible, narrative, ordinary, representational, metaphorical, epiphanic, formally predictable. Versus Rosemary Aubert's characterization of the field as dominated by non-accessible, non-commercial poetry, Good outlines what he calls a new aesthetic trend:

Not all poetry is difficult. One of the biggest trends in contemporary poetry
... has been the rise of anecdotal poetry that speaks in plain language about
everyday occurrences. It usually presents a slice of life rounded off with a
metaphor (this is poetry, after all) that comes in at the end like a punch
line. We might call it observational poetry, composed in the spirit of a Sein-
feld monologue, but usually not as funny. ("Americana")

Exactly when Good locates the recent "rise" of this poetry is unclear,
since what he describes is, by all appearances, precisely what postmod-
ern poetries have rejected since the early 1960s.

    Crafts discourse tends to either figure poetry in the direction of a util-
itarian text-object, or in the direction of the text-object of value-as-value
abstracted through a process of utilitarian labour. In this schema, poetic
knowledge can't be a speculative form of knowledge. Poetic knowledge
has to be a set of skills, techniques. Versus the poetic postmodern recon-
ceptions of poetry as epistemology, proposed by precursors like Laura
Riding and Charles Olson, carried forward by poets like Susan Howe,
Lyn Heijinian and Lissa Wolsak (among others), as crafts knowledge
poetic knowledge is essentially skill in persuasion. Seduction. Rhetoric.
Direction. This is visible in a review of Mari-Lou Rowley's book *Viral*
Suite. In a short passage, Katia Grubisic, author of *what if red ran out*
(which won a Gerald Lampert Award), moves away from the concept of
poetry as speculative knowledge operant in Rowley's book, to caution
Rowley against rakish cerebration. Grubisic effectively cautions Rowley
against writing poetry without predefined goals:

Science and poetry both try to fathom the universe, to come to terms,
through physics and metaphysics respectively, with the paradox that we
humans can experience finite portions of the infinite. Artistically, the com-
bination is tempting: science is brimming with good metaphors. Science ...
astounds with its symmetry, its connectedness, the way even curved lines

lead somewhere and affect other lines. Poetry, too, hinges on relationships and intersections; language receives energy, changes course, discovers its potential. The danger with poetry, however, as my father likes to say, is that if you don't know where you're going, you might very well end up somewhere else. ("Viral")

In her initial positive comparison of poetry with scientific knowledge, Grubisic articulates an almost Creeleyian poetics, the one resituated in Canada by poets like George Bowering and Fred Wah. "Language receives energy:" form emerges from the practice of attentiveness to language's confluent mechanics, attentiveness to what Grubisic calls language's "potential." In such poetics, the poet author may be as surprised as any reader at what emerges. But to Grubisic's restrictive aesthetic conscience, indeterminate cerebration is only poetically licit if some guarantee is felt throughout that the "curved lines lead somewhere" definite. The party must have a scheduled end. Rationalist aesthetic conscience intercedes with the stern caution that, in poetry, curvy lines might not lead towards sure destinations. Aesthetic conscience asks, through the phantasm of Grubisic's father: Careful, my daughter, do you know where you're going? The question of postmodern poetry is: Why would it be dangerous to end up "somewhere else" in poetic composition? Why should the poet should know the goal before starting the process? What is the risk? What perils? They only risk is that ideologies of poetic value will be challenged by the poetry that results. The aesthetic conscience of many Canadian poetry reviewers can only tolerate a narrow margin of negative capability in a poet – too much puts him/her at risk of making the wrong poems, poems that cannot be addressed in the dominant ideolect.

A Guild of Craftsman Scientists (with Magical Secrets)

The definition of poetry and the poet's social role is a core stake in the positions struggles within the divided field of Canadian poetry. To define the social role of poetry is to delimit the poetic field as such, to stake out what positions are licitly available to actors. It is to determine what Bourdieu terms the "space of possibles" (*Rules* 234). For poets in Canada, the postmodern turn alters the sociality of poetry in a way that intensifies such definitional struggles, further dividing the field. To define the space of possibles is to draw the limits of what is licit to desire in/of poetry, and, so, what kinds of texts can legitimately circulate under its sign. For Bourdieu: "at stake is the power to impose the dominant definition of the writer ... the *boundary* of the field is a stake of struggles" (*Field* 42). This, in turn, entails definition of what type of cultural labour poetic labour is. What is the job of the poet? Bourdieu observes correctly that poetry "is the arena *par excellence* of struggles over job definition" (*Field* 62). Poetry reviewers continue to trip over the axial question: What does poetry do? This rests on the deeper question: What is poetry? The latter is itself an answer to the question: What form of work does a poet do?

Poetry (and art at large) is often a cultural cipher for the acute collective longing for unalienated forms of work. When Frederic Jameson analyzes the figure of the scientist in sci-fi in "Towards Dialectical Criticism," he discovers projections of that longing:

These works ... rather openly express the mystique of the scientist: and by that I refer ... to a kind of collective folk-dream about the life-style of the scientist himself: he doesn't do real work (yet power is his and social status as well), his remuneration is not monetary or at the very least money seems no object, there is something fascinating about his laboratory (the home workshop magnified to institutional dimensions, a combination of factory and clinic), about the way he works nights (he isn't bound by routine or the eight-hour day).... There is, moreover, the suggestion of a return to older modes of work organization: to the more personal and psychologically sat-isfying world of the guilds, in which the older scientist is the master and the younger one the apprentice, in which the daughter of the older man becomes naturally enough the symbol of the transfer of functions. And so forth: these traits may be indefinitely enumerated and elaborated. What I want to convey is that ultimately none of this has anything to do with science itself, but is rather a distorted reflection of our own feelings and dreams about work alienated and nonalienated: it is a wish-fulfilment that takes as its object a vision of ideal or what Marcuse would call 'libidinally gratifying' work. (62 emphases in original)

Such "folk dreams" about the labour of the special person (scientist, art genius, poet, etc.) are an orienting component of poetry reviewers' aesthetic consciences, and of Canadian cultural ideology at large. Field-wide, the folky labour fantasy spans both the division within Canadian poetry and broader art-disciplinary divisions. Art (as phantasmic trope) serves partly as an object fetish of the common dream of freedom from the exploitative reality of the capitalist wage-contract. These agonistic, sublimated hopes relate directly to those expressed elsewhere as gam-bling addictions, the mania for lotteries, and celebrity worship. Poetry has long experienced a constant (internal) crisis of self-justification (there are countless defences of poetry in the history of poetics), a crisis intensified in the current long neoliberal cultural moment, when every social practice is under pressure to justify itself in brute fiscal terms. In one sense, reviewers try to construct poetry as a form of labour ethically defensible within a neoliberal, economist value ideology. For the same reason, they also use reviews to shame poets to "get a real job" – to write poetry in a way that represents poetry as both a morally and economically defencible form of labour.

For poetry as work to be consciable in these terms – for the poet-worker to gain aesthetico-moral innocence or capitalist absolution – it has to be possible for poets and their poet-reviewers to imagine themselves in a distinctive solidarity with other workers. Just resentment, just hatred of alienated labour, or the desire for alternative categories of human value, are sources of guilt. (If poets should "slave" over line endings, as Shane Neilson says, the Boss of an economistic aesthetic conscience holds the editorial whip.) Yet the Poet, like the celebrity, is also a phantasm of a subject liberated from alienated work. Like the scientist of science fiction Jameson describes, therefore, he/she is a special, non-alienated worker. The poet is not figured as one of the losers of capitalism (not a line cook at Wendy's, nor a recyclables binner), but as a specialized, sometimes elite, skilled worker: Plumber, artisan, scientist, athlete, scholar, sculptor, blacksmith, wordsmith. As R.J. MacSween, poet and Catholic priest who co-founded *The Antigonish Review*, writes: "Scattered throughout the volume are these short, finely worked passages, poems of painter and carver" (102). Economically consciable, productive toil, that is yet libidinally gratifying. When a notion of pleasure finds its way into the base categories of a reviewer's ideolect, it is most often the pleasure of the Sabbath – virtuous delectation fully earned in the restraints of sweaty diligence.

In 2005, *Brick* magazine published a poetics statement by Don Paterson (author of numerous collections, and appointed, in 2008, Officer of the Order of the British Empire) called "The Dark Art of Poetry," premised on confidently job-essentialist statements about poetry as labour. Mournful of senses of solidarity, cultural pertinence, and confident identity, which Paterson fantasizes poets had in *Simpler Times,* he argues that poets could recreate these conditions through neo-guildhood. Paterson's guild of poets is a curious hybrid of peer-reviewed science, artisanal guild, and occult priesthood:

Only plumbers can plumb, roofers roof, and drummers drum. Only poets can write poetry. Restoring the science of verse-making might restore our self-certainty in this matter, and naturally resurrect a guild that would soon find it had some secrets worth preserving. (21)

Initially, Paterson associates poetry with skilled manual work, with craftsmanship or skilled labour, rather than bookish, highbrow, or abstract sedentary toil. Paterson does not write that only geneticists gene, only academics academe, only psychologists psych. To regain economic dignity, the poet becomes a type of worker among other skilled workers, far from the twin abjections of brutal factory labour or abstracted office labour. Nor, however, does Paterson allow that a poet can be both plumber and poet at the same time. The poet cannot be an interdisciplinarian; a total fusion of job with a unitary aesthetic identity is requisite, as the poet is also a religious or magical worker of vocation. To restore the "science of verse-making" would be to regain the powers that supposedly once gave poets the occult, mesmeric power of a priesthood. Poets' secrets, their practical rhetorical skills, their science, would be aimed at nothing except producing value for poetry through its irrational (libidinal) veneration. Poet, be like a celebrity! In an art-sociological sense, Paterson is not mistaken. As Bourdieu writes:

[T]he power of the magician is a legitimate imposture, *collectively misrecognised, and hence recognised ... [Similarly] the work of art, like religious goods or services, amulets or various sacraments, receives value only from collective belief as collective misrecognition, collectively produced and reproduced.* (Rules 169-72)

Yes, if poets want a secure paycheque, rather than operate as a critical social practice, or an exploratory epistemology, poetry must aspire to become an apparatus of deceit, a no-budget spiritual spectacular. Paterson's magical science guild has these demagogic implications, and suggests furthermore a closed circle of members with absolute regulatory power to decide which products are honoured with the name of poetry, and which cultural workers merit initiation.

One underlying premise of the reviewers' ideolect is that linguistic communication is expression. The expressive/communcative paradigm of meaning requires not only, as Michael Davidson critiques, that "poetry exists to reflect the poet's mind as he or she comes to grips with political and social contradictions" (143), but that poetic meaning is an expression of something other than, and something formulated prior to (rather than something produced in, inseparable from), the poem. Although reviewers often write sandwiched abstractions in sentences such as: "His craft is extremely well polished," the notion extends backwards from the cultural product to that legendary place of toil, and to the poet. The (imagined) work activity expresses the vocational identity of the worker. Form is the vehicle or vessel of a message, a prior content – that content is often the poet him/herself.

Yes, the fact that poets like Milton Acorn, David Huggett, Ken Babstock, Patrick Lane, and Kate Braid, not to mention Jesus Christ, worked as carpenters is often taken to help explain their writing/working ethos and the form of their poetry. The scrupulous work habits such poets must have acquired as carpenters are, supposedly, transferred to their work as verse-makers. Aesthetic reasoning elaborates this analogy a long way from its initial root analogy of POETRY IS CRAFT. In 1990, George Woodcock praises the quality of Milton Acorn's poetic craftsmanship through an extended analogy to carpentry. Because the analogy is rooted in biographical fact, it takes on an irrefutable, common sense character:

the sense of fine crafting that in another aspect of his life we are told char-
acterised his work as a good carpenter. There is no loose jointing, either
verbal or intellectual in his finished poetry ... no real incoherence, every-
thing fits. (102)

A central component of Woodcock's argument his assertion of the qual-
ity of Acorn's poetry by reference to Acorn's credibility as a normal
economic actor. Acorn, the poet, is credited for having been economi-
cally productive before he took up poetry. A masculine master in both
spheres, Acorn did not turn to poetry from sloth, unemployment or
incompetence. What Woodcock values as tight "verbal or intellectual"
jointing, or coherence, thus gains a positive moral resonance within the
terms of an economist work ethic. Acorn brings home the poetic ba-
con, as it were, and so aesthetic conscience is permitted quiet admiration
of this poetry. Over a decade later, Zachariah Wells discovers the same
workman/craftsman ethos in an all-male group of poets including Ken
Babstock, Pete Trower, Joe Denham, Peter Richardson and Adam Getty.

These five poets have markedly distinct voices and techniques for approach-
ing manual labour as a subject of their poetry. What they share is a com-
mitment to their readers and to the art of poetry itself. This commitment
consists ... of a resistance to literary preciousness and self-indulgent esoter-
ic obscurity and an emphasis on craft and shared humanity.... As workers
themselves, they respect a job well done and the work that goes into a finely
forged tool or weapon. ("Makin' It")

A crafts guild must regulate the products that bear its stamp, to protect
its cultural and economic capital. To this end, aesthetic conscience can
morally bribe itself into believing it works with an inductive objectivity,
while it actually abstracts its standards of quality from poetry it first judg-
es intuitively as good. (Rationalization often comes later in the sequence
of conscience.) As reviewers often do, Wells here defines, in negative and

positive terms, what he believes poetry is. Like Woodcock above, who grants value to Acorn's poetry because of its apparent work ethic, Wells equates a work-ethical imperative with an actual definition of poetry: "commitment to their readers," or commitment to the Common Reader. Because these men were true workers in the past, they have virtuous aesthetic morality, and what they produce is true poetry. In particular they respect the "work that goes into a finely forged tool or weapon." Not the effeminate jewellery of "literary preciousness," the sinful onanism of the "self-indulgent," nor the soft-skinned hands of "esoteric obscurity." Poetry's value is in (specifically) instrumental utility. Poetry is a weapon or a tool. In reviews such as Wells', a morality of labour produces the fetish of true poetry. Poetry is valued as the product of an ethically correct labour, as such. As Roland Barthes writes: "Writing is now to be saved not by virtue of what it exists for, but what it has cost." Barthes, and reviewers like Wells, echo Marx in *Capital*: "As values, all commodities are only definite masses of congealed labour time." (15) Tom Wayman correctly observed the "taboo [in Can Lit] against accurately depicting daily work" (118), yet in the ideology of Canadian poetry reviews that suppressed work vengefully returns in a variety of powerful, sublimated forms.

Secretary of Smash the State

Some influential, provocative articulations of position made by US-American poet Kenneth Goldsmith are through redefinitions of the type of work that poetry is, and the type of work a poet does. Goldsmith's critical writing continues to attract controversy in Canada and the USA, partly by how his re-figuration of the idiomatic labour of the poet challenges the discourse of craft. Rather than a specialized virtuous labourer or artisan, Goldsmith's poetic worker is a hybrid of wage slave and outlaw. He writes that:

[C]ontemporary writing requires the expertise of a secretary crossed with the attitude of a pirate: replicating, organizing, mirroring, archiving, and reprinting, along with a more clandestine proclivity for bootlegging, plundering, hoarding, and file-sharing. We've needed to acquire a whole new skill set: we've become master typists, exacting cut-and-pasters, and OCR demons…. There is no museum or bookstore in the world better than our local Staples. The writer's solitary lair is transformed into a networked alchemical laboratory, dedicated to the brute physicality of textual transference. ("Information Management")

Goldsmith's counter-romantic poet here makes him/her something like an embezzler, with the skills and insider knowledge of the secretary and opportunist morality of a pirate. Goldsmith's poet has a pirate's eye for opportunities of cultural context that can be "seized" through the long drudgery of menial informatic tasks. His poet is not a scrupulous watchmaker; he/she shovels linguistic compost from one context to another. Writing is the "brute physicality of textual transference" involved in moving found texts into contexts where they will be read aesthetically. While a secretary is a highly skilled but servile, information-management wage worker, the pirate is an economic parasite. Neither are economically productive as such, unlike, say, a carpenter or potter, blacksmith, painter or carver, who produce substantial goods for sale. A secretary (merely) manages information, produces nothing new. The pirate, an anarchistic outcast, steals, scavenges, or eats carrion. In spite of the secretary's high level of skill, neither can he/she hope for the *it's-a-job-well-done!* end of the day moment of the satisfied artisan. This very alienation is part of what makes him/her a potential interloper, a risk of turning pirate/embezzler. Both might be believed, prejudicially, by mercantile aesthetic conscience, to be basically lazy.[16] The secretary is forced to work extremely hard, yet may be believed to lack the virtuous self-motivation (basic spiritual diligence) of the craftsman. A pirate personifies out-and-out carnal sloth and appetite become sheer criminality. Goldsmith also shifts the fantasy site of poetry away from the legendary places of exquisite toil or sublime craftsmanship, away from the great museum of the Tradition. Rather than a literary museum (legendary past achievements, sacred objects, a materialized body of knowledge), a Staples store, as the site of poetry production, suggests the culturally nihilist amnesia of corporate capitalism. Not accidentally, Goldsmith figures the fantasy site of "contemporary writing" – antagonistic to poetry even in name – as a warehouse-sized space full of cheap office supplies, blank paper and computer hardware.

Goldsmith's ultra-postmodern poet is categorically antagonistic to the poet of crafts discourse. This antagonism is not only a question of the employment obligations of the craftsman poet, but of the obligatory

---

16 Recall, in this context, the racist stereotype of the *lazy slave*.

aesthetic identification of poet with the form of labour poetry is, and with its ethos. The fuller harmonizations of aesthetic conscience performed in some reviews require that this identification be total. Morality of the job becomes equivalent to the morality of the jobber. From this identification, mediated by the assumption that poetry expresses preformulated meanings, the form of the poetry under review takes on sharp moral significance. Reviewers often make judgements as if a living poet's entire morality can be inferred from his/her compositional decisions. These inferences sometimes slide into *ad hominem*. The book of poetry judged as bad must have been written by a bad person, if not a morally ill person. The book of good poems is the work of someone ultimately good (even if "flawed"), aesthetically virtuous, Human. Assumptions about the relationship of work and value further ground this chain of identifications, both in that labour turns into a poetic value fetish, and that, consequently, labour as such ritualistically (magically) imparts value to an object. To make such value discursively legible, however, it has to be possible for reviewers to frame certain features of poetry as the legible, obvious traces of good labour. Without a reciprocating gaze, the value is never realized, never concretely enters the cultural field. As David Ormsby characterises a poet's life: "Hard work, little recognition" ("Poet's Life"). The poet peers into a void.

In "Conscience Doth Make Subjects of Us All," both a critique and vindication of Althusser's theory of interpellation, Judith Butler finds in "the lived simultaneity of submission and mastery" (15) a crucial point of transfer between the logic of accumulation and the skilled labourer's work ethic. Among the premises that ground the morality of aesthetic labour in the crafts discourse of poetry reviewing are residual Christian notions of sin and innocence. Butler argues that:

The reproduction of social relations, the reproduction of skills, is the reproduction of subjection, but here it is not the reproduction of labor [sic] that is central, but a reproduction proper to the subject, one that takes place in relation to language *and to the formation of conscience. For Althusser, to perform tasks 'conscientiously' is to perform them … again and again, to reproduce those skills, and in reproducing them, acquire mastery. 'Conscientiously' is placed in quotation marks … thus bringing in to relief the way in which labor is moralized.… If the mastery of a set of skills is to be construed [as Althusser does] as an* acquitting of oneself, *this mastery … will constitute a defense of oneself against an accusation, or, quite literally, a declaring of innocence on the part of the accused. To acquit oneself 'conscientiously' of one's task is, then, to construe labor as a confession of innocence, a display or proof of guiltlessness in the face of the demand for confession implied by an insistent accusation.* (16)

In poetry reviewing, the "insistent accusation" levelled is of writing bad poetry. However the poetry in question is finally judged, the redeeming, answering confession is that *poetry is hard to write* and *I have worked hard at writing this poetry.* A poet can only pre-emptively acquit him/herself by building into his/her poetry features which appear to signify the hard work it cost to write. In the consciences of some reviewers, diligence almost comes to equal quality. The formula is: work harder = write better. Aesthetic conscience, in these terms, must forcefully maintain the assumption (verifiable or not) that good poetry is difficult to write. An entire mode of value would collapse if it ever emerges that poetry is easy to write, or if poetry somehow (by computerized automation, for example) becomes easy to write. Ultimately, poetry has to appear to have been difficult to write in order to be judged good.[17]

Deeply implicated in poetry's endless "crisis of self-justification" is the mystery of how exchange value accrues to cultural objects. The symbolic value of a cultural practice like poetry (somehow prestigious yet without

---

17 Difficulty is often inferred from the sprezzatura of the virtuoso: i.e., "she makes it look so easy.…" Actual practitioners may take virtuosic ease as a sign of intensive, long rehearsal.

significant remuneration) is not easily translatable into economist terms of exchange value. Yet, with economism as a cultural dominant, ideological pressures to make that difficult translation are one of the motivators in the reviewer's aesthetic conscience. The solution many turn to is the "declaration of innocence" made to economist morality through this valuation of writerly labour, as an attempt to translate the insubstantial *illusio* of poetry (as language) into that of capitalist economics. Here, as Barthes says, "labour replaces genius as a value." The poetry is better because the poet worked harder; the social constitution of culture is reified to representations of individual exertion, effort, strain. The field vanishes from view, along with the concrete struggles that constitute the whole historical process of value creation. As Robert Lowell wrote so backhandedly to Theodore Roethke: "One of the things I marvel at in your poems is the impression they give of having been worked on an extra half day" (qtd. in McClatchy xxiii). At a not too rare extreme, reviews treat the poem-object as if it stores labour energy like a rechargeable battery, inadvertently reproducing something like the labour theory of value. As Marx writes in *Capital*:

A use value ... has value only because human labour in the abstract has been embodied or materialised in it. How, then, is the magnitude of this value to be measured? Plainly, by the quantity of the value-creating substance, the labour, contained in the article. The quantity of labour, however, is measured by its duration, and labour time in its turn finds its standard in weeks, days, and hours. (15)

To the degree that this value accumulates through labour, the poet buys his/her innocence, buys quietude of aesthetic conscience. Poets who receive negative reviews can reassure themselves that, in spite of all that, they worked hard, they did their best.

While poetry reviewers often articulate their adjudicative mandate as a guild-protecting practice of quality control, reviewing more often functions like a work ethical Neighbourhood Watch. The actual poet is assumed slothful until proven diligent. Immoral, slothful poetry is expelled from the definition of poetry. As Byron wrote of Keats's poetry, "[it is] neither poetry nor any thing else but a Bedlam vision produced by raw pork and opium" (qtd. in McFarland 107). Common descriptors like "excessive," "too much," "too often," are moral excoriations. The poet fails to exercise the impassioned restraint through which value and absolution can be seen to steadily accrue. In a review of Anne Glickman, Anita Lahey, author of *Out to Dry in Cape Breton*, demonstrates the processes of this work-burdened aesthetic conscience in motion. Lahey is initially puzzled about what she judges as the unevenness of Glickman's poetry. She then engages in some serious aesthetic reasoning, turning to other reviewers to construct a collective phantasmic panel of Expert Readers that can confirm her already-formed intuitions about Glickman's aesthetic morality. Glickman, she concludes, is in sin: She hasn't worked hard enough. Lahey polarizes the logic of work (as productive accumulation and moral acquittal), against play (as wasteful expenditure and immorality):

I look up Glickman's old reviews. I want to know how she was read when she came on the scene…. I find her … praised more than criticized. But I also encounter references to weak line breaks, to a cadence 'a bit too colloquial, a bit too Purdyish'…. M. Travis Lane suggests that Glickman gets into trouble when she tackles weighty subjects: 'the lightness of her tone is a problem'…. Reading Running *through to the end, I conclude that Glickman is too comfortable. She is enjoying herself, her rhythms and insights, but a little too much, a little more than she has earned…. She has not been tough enough on herself to realise her own poetic potential. (83)*

Lahey's moral qualms drift in through the cracks, like the odour of scandal. Features like "weak line breaks" are moralized form – line breaks that don't do enough work. Soon Lahey makes moral insinuations in the form of a discourse of manners; her lassitude in being "a bit too col-loquial" evinces a lack of moral fibre. The argument is reminiscent of those who misappropriate the term "formal" to mean something very close to "formality," as in "formal dress," rather than an investigation of the problems related to literary form. So "the lightness of her tone is a problem" because "weighty subjects" require a prosodic suit and tie, cor-rect discursive manners and an air of high-mindedness. If Glickman is "too comfortable," her aesthetic conscience is weak; she is inadequately "tough on herself." In terms of the logic of value accumulation through work, Glickman has not laboured hard enough to have "earned" plea-sure by accruing the poetic quality with which to purchase that pleasure. Hard work is a basic condition for writing poetry of excellence, for real-izing "poetic potential" – like economic earning potential.

When a poet like Glickman above, appears to a reviewer to be "just playing" or is "not serious," even if the reviewer endorses the book, it can only accrue a severely limited amount of value. Comical poetry is thus valued by most reviewers on a lower scale. Comic poetry is too much fun, cannot have cost the writer enough virtue calories to be of supreme quality or importance. It remains of a lesser order than earnest, high-minded poetry of the Big Affective Moment. Nietzsche argues in *Daybreak* that this imperative of conscience emerges directly from a reptile pleasure humans derive from seeing others suffer. To Nietzsche, the foundation of moralities of discipline and privation is basic human cruelty. Virtuous work, in this schema, is a painful sacrifice that "steams up to [the evil gods] like a perpetual propitiatory sacrifice on the altar" (138). Most pertinent in his argument is the observation that the more the boundaries and terms of morality are extended, the more impera-tive such privation becomes, and the more virtue it accrues. Although too essentialist, Nietzsche's reflection helps explain why more Thomas Gradgrinds and Hard Hearts exist among Canadian poetry reviewers today than 50 years ago. Insistent challenges to dominant poetic values emerge from multiple directions since 1961. From postmodern poetry and equally from identitarian writing practices (e.g., feminist writing, racialized writing, justice writing) that sometimes programmatically ignore the entire historical, institutional and ideological bases of reviewers' adjudicative authority. These challenges force an intensification of position, a digging-in, which stokes the righteous flames. Nietzsche writes:

The more their spirit ventured on to new paths and was as a consequence tormented by pangs of conscience and spasms of anxiety, the more cruelly did they rage against their own flesh, their own appetites and their own health – as though to offer the divinity a substitute pleasure. (138)

Laziness is now the ultimate immorality in a poet, worse than masturbatory (sinful) self-indulgence. Hard work is the poet's responsibility, the imperative of efficacious aesthetic conscience. So Carole Langille, author of three poetry collections, is relieved to find that poet Adam Sol's "is a world deeply felt, where responsibility is not taken lightly" (124). In the same vein, Brian Fawcett fumes, getting into good odour with the capitalist gods, in a 1978 review-article "The Conditions of Poetry in Canada:"

I don't know what goes into a reversal of metaphor that leads someone to prefer abstractions like those in the last two lines quoted except to recognise the profound reactionary nature of it. The forms of expression are also reactionary – & by that I don't mean the presence of sonnets. Both reactions are symtoms [sic] of a fundamental laziness in their work. They take the easiest possible esplanation [sic] of their condition, & [sic] the condition of contemporary poetry – it's all a trick…. The assumption these people make, I suspect, is that poetry & life is [sic] so incomprehensible that it is to be met with tricks – sleight of hand, mind or whatever – to keep the show going. (1978 no pagination)

Fawcett still associates himself, in this phase of his career, with postmodern tendencies in poetry. Before he comes out aggressively against what he calls Language Centred Writing, Fawcett's own work appears in $L=A=N=G=U=A=G=E$ magazine. His positional concordances with other reviewers above are therefore distinctive. Although Fawcett writes from a professedly Leftist position against "reactionary" poetry, he asks the same *ad hominem* question, based on untestable inferences about the poet's morality and character. Fawcett asks not: What are the abstractions doing in these poems? Instead, he asks: What sort of person would prefer abstractions? Fawcett then flings a glass of the most morally corrosive poet-to-poet insult: an accusation of laziness. When he finds, however, that these reactionary sonneteers indeed appear to spend a lot of concrete time tinkering in the legendary place of craft, aesthetic conscience adapts its terms, changes the definitions. Whatever they do when meticulously counting syllables, scanning metrics and substituting robust nouns for flowery adjectives is not real work, only "tricks – sleight of hand." To deliver the mortal insult, conscience shifts its attention from surface signs of laziness (which it fails to find) to the depth register of a "fundamental laziness." It may look like they are working hard, but they are not *really* working hard: They camouflage sloth with a masquerade of diligence. When faced with the incomprehensible, these poets deflate rather than take up the burden of solemn duty. As an immoral set, they resort to obfuscation, to poetic spectacle for its own vain sake, "to keep the show going." (Note that in this way Fawcett defines a position directly antagonistic to the occult priest scientific poetry guild proposed by Don Paterson above.)

Drawing his from several sources, including Bataille, Barthes and Bourdieu, Steve McCaffery in "Writing as a General Economy," articulates of how a notion of play in extremis might help open the "restricted economy" of this literary ideology. McCaffery begins from a familiar postmodern inversion of normative poetic values (play valued over work), then progresses to a more radical critique. He breaks apart the simplistic dichotomy that might be drawn, for example, from Barthes' rather direct inversion of values (against work in favour of play.)

Restricted economy, which is the economy of Capital, Reason, Philosophy, and History, will always strive to govern writing, to force its appearance through an order of constraints. The general economy would forfeit this government, conserve nothing, and, while not prohibiting meaning's appearance, would only sanction its profitless emergence in general expenditure: hence, it would be entirely indifferent to results and concerned only with self-dispersal. A general economy can never be countervaluational nor offer an alternative 'value' to Value, for it is precisely the operation of value that it explicitly disavows. (202)

In terms of the further poet-customer agreement implicit in craft discourse, the poet who hasn't worked hard enough, who has merely doodled, scribbled, idled, masturbated or played with words – what McCaffery characterizes as "general expenditure," or "nonproductive outlay" (207) – has no moral right to ask for the Common Reader's time. In this same vein, John Baglow, author of two poetry collections and a study of Scottish socialist poet Hugh MacDiarmid, holds out the possibility of forgiveness to playful poet Mark Truscott:

There is not enough in [this book] for a real night on the town.... Instead we have page after page of what can only be described as verbal doodling.... But luckily this is not all there is to Truscott.... Sometimes, as above, this is just the flash and dash of an enthusiast taken with his own discoveries, but when the frivolous mood wears off, he proves to be capable of much more.... 'Canadian Poetry' is proof that he can do far more than play with words.... If Truscott can abandon the self-indulgence of "It Was," and give us instead the more lucid and compelling contents of his mind's "succession of torn envelopes," that night on the town will be well worth waiting for. ("Said Like Reeds")

Baglow initially allows for possible temptation (against his aesthetic conscience) to a poetic night on the town, before he decides Truscott has not been cruel enough to his own flesh to conscionably purchase rest. Truscott's writing does not demonstrate often enough the ideologically legible signs of toil, and therefore most of it is categorically not poetry. Instead his poetry "can only be described as verbal doodling:" undirected semantic play, speculation, discovery. Rather than see the root problem as their incompatibility of poetic values, or their divergent aesthetic imperatives, Baglow slanderously infers that Truscott is not a serious character. Truscott's affects – frivolity, playfulness, enthusiasm, self-love – are not those of virtuous, responsible poetry. Baglow seems to believe Truscott was either high on marijuana, and/or Prozac (either way: temporary moral insanity!), when the book was put together, in a speedy "flash and dash," or that he is immoral because he is still immature (i.e., he has not yet formed an aesthetic conscience). But Baglow's poetry science church guild nevertheless prays for poets like Truscott, with whom some hope remains, because "luckily … [they] can do far more than play with words." Truscott, in the end, is compassionately encouraged to be strong, to grow up, to put away childish things.

Stuart Newton, in the same review cited above, takes a more severe adjudicative position:

These books disappoint the reader in a fashion that is peculiar to contemporary theories of poetry: vis-à-vis free verse and concrete forms. Worthwhile poetry requires much more than verbal and graphic stimuli. Unconcerned, the three writers plopped down their lines produced their graphics in three rather showy texts…. All this poor work occurs because Fertig has no sound notion of poetics…. Fertig's random symbol scheme demands that the reader be the poet, in that the reader has to fuse together some sort of cohesion from such disparity…. [Varney's] book is not a serious proposition…. Poetry is not a free whim, it is a persistent vision that drives the poet to his pen and paper…. Poetry, then, is much more than a reasonable account of a passing moment: it is very serious work. Good poems are not just chance…. It is easy to hoax readers when they are meant to be open

to Vers Libre, even easier when the readers are made to be the poet so that
they are disinclined to judge. (Rev. of Fertig, Rappaport and Varney 142)

Newton, outraged, spurs to a strong position-taking in a stringently
moralised definition of poetry. As reviewers will, Newton shames the
actual persons (not the author-functions, nor the fantasmic Poets) Fer-
tig, Rappaport and Varney. His very parental Common Reader expresses
the moral-narrative emotion of disappointment: I thought you would
do better. He defines poetry specifically as a work ethic, not by reference
to form or content. "Poetry is not a free whim … it is a persistent vision
… it is very serious work." *Vers enchainé*, not *vers libre*. In this scheme,
all of postmodern poetry, and, it would seem, most poetry of the 20th
century, is the hoax of con-artist writers whose works turn readers away
from the honourable duty of judgement, in order to hide their chicanery.
Such "unconcerned" poets are disturbingly unburdened with aesthetic
conscience. They limply plop down their lines without design, and let
the reader do the work of symbolic re-assembly, a labour ghoulishly in-
tended to sap the Common Reader's passion for whack-a-mole gavel-
banging. "Worthwhile" here, as elsewhere, imagines the relationship be-
tween reader and writer in economic terms, as an exchange of readerly
time for writerly goods. Newton's parental reader is also an angry Tough
Customer, cheated of cohesion-as-value. A Tough Customer, no less,
who has to assemble the product him/herself. Reviewers like Newton
instrumentalize poetic value: A poem is good because it does something
definite, pointed, obvious. What apparently good poetry really does, for
a reviewer like Newton, is to signal accrued labour value in the correct
ideological code. Ideological features, such as cohesion, function as a
signs that the poet is not an aesthetic welfare bum, but that he/she works
for a poetic living.

7 Hours 7 Days 7 Years

In this context it is instructive to consider the marketing and critical reception of Christian Bök's 2001 book *Eunoia*. By its unmatched popularity alone,[18] *Eunoia* has greatly expanded the room for institutional recognition and reproductive potential of postmodern poetry in Canada. *Eunoia*'s success as such (more directly than its content or as a formal model) alters the topography of the Canadian poetic field more than that of any other single book published since the 1970s.[19] From the start, *Eunoia*'s reception in reviews, positive and negative, is dominated by the discourse of craft, with an acute focus on labour as value. This effect is partly by design of the poet and publisher. The marketing of the book plays on the terms of the dominant evaluative ideolect, and plays directly on the place of work in reviewers' aesthetic consciences. Before a single copy reaches bookstores, a legend of *Eunoia*'s impossibly arduous making has already been constructed.

---

18 In 2007 Eunoia had sold an estimated 20,000 copies, and in 2012 continues to sell, including an edition for the UK market – this compared to 200-300 copies total for an average book of Canadian poetry.
19 Note that only in 2011 does the Canada council finally acknowledge the existence of a historical division in the literary field, through the sorely belated introduction of the category "exploratory writing" in its program of Grants for Professional Writers. It defines "exploratory writing" as: "writing that uses technology to present literature in an innovative manner and (or) explores forms of literature outside the conventions of the novel, short story or poem."

First, the extreme formal constraint against which the book is written is straightforwardly material enough to boil down to the brevity of a Hollywood pitch. As reviewer Patty Osborne relates: "*Eunoia* is divided into five chapters, one for each of the five vowels, and each chapter tells an outlandish story written with words that contain only that vowel" (Rev. of Bök.). An extremely difficult writerly task to accomplish, readers learn before they buy or read the book, that the poet worked 7 hours per day 7 days per week for 7 years [or was it "four or five hours," as Robert Stacey quotes Bök saying? ("Toil" 65)] to write *Eunoia*. Immediately the frameworks of skill, mastery, labour, difficulty, diligence are invoked, and, in a negative reflection, the exploitative conditions of the wage contract. The author performs for the Common Reviewer of Canadian poetry exactly the phantasmic figure of the writer that Barthes draws, the writer who

shuts himself away in some legendary place, like a workman operating at home and who roughs out, cuts, polishes, and sets his form exactly as a jeweller extracts art from his material, devoting to his work regular hours of solitary effort. (Writing 63)

Eunoia is postmodern work in its construction and self-contextualisation within the poetic field. The book is postmodern in the sense that it self-consciously re-stages a high modernist compositional strategy as a book-trade high media event, postmodern in its invention and realization of its own strict formal procedure, and postmodern in the sense of pseudo-humanist reviewers who find it utterly "cynical" in its lack of moral affect, lack of authorial voice, and lack of (Accessible) philosophical reflection on the human condition. Yet *Eunoia* purchases, by a legend of labour, an incomparable moral innocence and fetishistic value within the permamodern linguistic economy, a depth of innocence most postmodern books can never afford.

 Eunoia is a socially complex proposition, which is what makes it an important book. Not that *Eunoia*, as Linda Hutcheon argues about much

Canadian postmodern fiction, "asserts and then deliberately undermines such principles as value, order, meaning, control and identity ... that have been the basic premises of bourgeois liberalism" (7). Rather, *Eunoia* simultaneously both confirms and disavows those premises on multiple levels. While being laborious and intricate in construction, its content is nihilist Dada comedy. To the dominant ideolect, *Eunoia*'s literary high-mindedness is entirely indexed in its valuation of labour, its meticulous verbal construction and its careful self-insertion into a chosen historical trajectory. Bök's labour, note, is the labour to magnificently surpass his predecessors in Oulipo, not to produce a severe historical rupture. As Bourdieu writes:

the presence of the specific past is most visible of all among the avant-garde producers who are controlled by the past when it comes to their intention to surpass it, an intention itself linked to a state of the history of the field.... It is ... the product of a disposition formed by the history of the field and informed by that history, and hence inscribed in the continuity of the field. (Rules 243)

But the monologic address of its symbolic package, its paratexts, that the book expresses "sublime thought" (i.e., continuous with dominant modes of value), contradicts the poem's devilishly absurdist content. To reviewers unwilling to read form, context, and historical position as di-mensions of a work's meaning, its content predictably reads like what they prudishly call "mental masturbation" (masturbation being a sinful habit of idle hands) or, in different terms, McCaffery's semiotic "general expenditure." Quoting *Eunoia* from "Chapter U:"

Ubu hugs Ruth; thus Ruth purrs. Ubu untucks Ruth's muumuu; thus Ruth must untruss Ubu's tux. Ubu fluffs Lulu's tutu. Ubu cups Lulu's dugs; Ubu rubs Lulu's buns; thus Lulu must pull Ubu's pud.... Ubu blurts: push push. Ubu thrusts. Ubu bucks. Cum spurts. Ubu cums. (79)

Robert Stacey ventures an eloquent defence of *Eunoia* in his essay "Toil and Trouble: On Work in Christian Bök's *Eunoia*," on the grounds of the symbolic role it gives to labour as exemplifying an optimistic, quasi-revolutionary "belief in the future" ("Toil" 76), a fierce struggle out towards freedom through the (symbolic) constraint of necessity. *Eunoia*, Stacey continues,

is work as a process of transformation, of appropriating and reshaping material nature, which brings the one realm to the threshold of the other and which connects the present to an as-yet-unrealised future. An idea of history as process is impossible without an idea of work because only work can bring about an end to its own necessity. ("Toil" 75)

Yet as a position-taking in the field of Canadian poetry, *Eunoia* cannot be complacently celebrated in this way. To do so is to make the same historical error as the Arnoldian-Leavisite critic whose aesthetic conscience compels him to find a morally salutary value in-and-of-itself in any work of art he judges outstanding, whatever its propositional content or political matrix. Stacey's reading of the potential social meaning of labour and form in *Eunoia* is not incorrect, just too virtuously partial, too programmatically liberal-Leftist. No: Art does not have to be morally, or politically good, to be good art. Instead, like the embezzler poet constructed by Kenneth Goldsmith, the poet of *Eunoia*'s legend, and the example of *Eunoia* as object, is deep in moral contradiction, staked in several incompatible social positions at once.

In the very least, as virtually every reviewer notes, the imperative of righteous labour, of working harder for poetic excellence, is absurdly overfilled in *Eunoia*. Reviewers convey frequently that *Eunoia* makes a "spectacle of its labour," quoting Bök's own pronouncement. *Eunoia* is compelled to make this spectacle by sheer structural pressures. As Bourdieu writes: "Art cannot deliver the truth about art without concealment, by turning this unveiling into an artistic manifestation" (*Rules* 169). Yet in content, *Eunoia* is an Alfred Jarry-esque book of boyish sci-fi nihilism and absurdist comedy. On the one hand, Bök's poet is the model poetry Stakhanovite, yet his other values, his aesthetico-moral imperatives, are wrong. Low-minded comedy of the kind in *Eunoia* is a mode of writing to which the dominant Canadian poetry reviewers' aesthetic conscience never ascribes supreme cultural value; to devote so much labour to (unserious) comedy is, in terms of the dominant ideolect, inherently wasteful.

Eunoia does make a spectacle of its labour, in various ways. Aside from its pre-packaging in legend, as Stacey notes, the

singing [in Eunoia*] takes place under duress, against a countermanding pressure that is registered in the language and structure of the sentences themselves which at every moment announce the effort that went into their production.* ("Toil" 66)

Further, as Stacey also identifies, numerous passages in the poem are about labour and craftsmanship. Aside from the first person sections about writing, several sections directly contradict the ejaculatory general expenditure passages of "Chapter U." In "Chapter I," for example:

Pilgrims, digging in shifts, dig till midnight in mining pits, chipping flint with picks, drilling schist with drills, striking it rich mining zinc. Irish firms, hiring micks whilst firing Brits, bring in smiths with mining skills: kilnwrights grilling brick in brickkilns, millwrights grinding grist in gristmills. Irish tinsmiths, fiddling with widgets, fix this rig, driving its drills which spin whirling drillbits. (67)

When they evaluate the product of this labour, *Eunoia*'s detractors are partially right that it demonstrates "Empty Productivity" (Starnino "Vowel Movements"). Yes, and it is precisely as "empty productivity" that *Eunoia* can "[register] as an implicit critique of global consumer culture"

225

(Stacey, "Toil" 66). It shows up ordinary wage-work as the exploitative brutality that it is, with neither belief in future emancipation or reflex nostalgia for Simpler Times. Were it written through the same constraints, but "filled" with the high-minded thematic content of official verse culture, the plane of that content would dominate its reception. As per usual, reviewers would be entirely off the hook about the significance of form, and set their focus on poetic vision, noble themes, memorable image content, salubrious moral lessons, etc. Labour-as-form would not be made spectacular, labour would not emerge as "a *trope* … [as part of] its manner of meaning as well as the key to its subject matter" (Stacey, "Toil" 66-7). Form, again, would be relegated to a passive role as vessel, or cordoned off as a separate interpretative/evaluative issue. In either case, when they transmit the legend, reviewers usually omit the keyword of Bök's frequently quoted pronouncement from the afterword to *Eunoia*:

[T]he text makes a Sisyphean spectacle of its labor, wilfully crippling its language in order to show that, even under such improbable conditions of duress, language can still express an uncanny, if not sublime, thought. (111-12)

Bök writes *Sisyphean* – the labour is anti-heroic, unproductive, absurd – yet reviewers often respond as if he writes *Herculean*. Through the legend of its labour, *Eunoia* satisfies the most crucial terms of entry, whereas its comically absurdist content mocks, with perfect malice, the demagogical pretentions of upper-middle-brow Canadian official verse culture. *Eunoia* at once satisfies and critiques the dominant ideology of the Canadian poetry review in its own terms.

It is not so significant that a labour legend about this book exists, it is that such a high proportion of all notices and reviews of the book retell the legend. Uncountable books have such legendary backgrounds. Poets like Margaret Avison, Robin Blaser and Jeff Derksen are famously patient, unprolific. Many books that took as long, and were as difficult to write as *Eunoia* will never sell a fraction as many copies. Many others far easier to write will sell many more. Yet even *Eunoia*'s most programmatically hostile reviewer Carmine Starnino recounts the exemplary tale of labour, skill, and determination:

How else explain the growing legend of its execution? Bök's slog through the OED, *the long evenings of revision, the seven years of toil. Sometimes we need to witness such self-punishing acts of technical adroitness to shake up our cherished idea of poetry as a muse-inspired sport…. What isn't silly … is the sedulous skill it took to write…. To give credit where credit is due, poets who can bring off this sort of thing aren't exactly thick on the ground here.* ("Vowel Movements")

Again, *Eunoia* is a socially complex proposition. Starnino values the labour evidenced for providing an acid purgative to the sentimentality of naïve muse-lovers. The focus of the positional antagonism is thus complicated by the fact of a shared ethos on one crucial point. As Stacey notes: "in oulipian practice an idea of writing as work displaces a model of poetic inspiration" ("Toil" 66). Starnino is categorically compelled to give *Eunoia* some accreditation in the dominant ideolect. An odour of cruel ritual, as Nietzsche and Barthes predict, wafts out of the diction in which Starnino constructs this accreditation: "self-punishment," "slog," "long evenings," "toil." The non-silly aspect of the poem, its innocence, is precisely what is purchased through long, long hours in the woodshed. Diligence is made righteous by what it costs in flesh. His "sedulous skill" is not silly. Hard-won skill is untheorizable, absolute, blood-and-guts value. The positional contrast Starnino makes in lines that follow confirm this point. With a lithe manoeuvre, Starnino affiliates himself with Bök's hard-won virtuosity (and elevates himself as reviewer and poet from the flabby rabble "thick on the ground"), but not with Bök's aesthetic conscience. Bök's imperatives are perversely beneath the aesthetic morality of homo-economicus-aestheticus represented by Starnino.

As in Starnino's review, the conscientious deliberation hinges on whether the "seven years of toil" were Sisyphean or Herculean. Supportive reviewers are careful to indicate that they believe the time was not wasteful expenditure (not Sisyphean, not empty productivity), but properly accumulative, heroic (Herculean). This is key: To its defenders, *Eunoia* stores so much magical labour energy that the sublime remains to eclipse the absurd. They don't seem to notice how insistently and pleasurably goofy it is. With his "sedulous skill" alone Bök can be constructed as a master craftsman. As Michel Basilieres declares in *The Danforth Review*: "The seven years of effort Bök poured into *Eunoia* have paid off…. It's not only one of the best books of the year; it's quite simply a masterpiece" (Rev. of Bök). In a snowblinding phrase such as "quite simply," obsolete categories of value assert themselves with a blunt force typical of the ideological. As in sullivan's review of Lionel Kearns above, categorically challenged by a new work, aesthetic conscience can expand the envelope of an old definition to achieve quiet. Yet if conscience thus finds reassurance, the price, once again, is the work's social, historical complexity. Calling *Eunoia* "simply a masterpiece" is a recuperative act of ideological mummification that freeze-dries the book for the museum shelves of Tradition, to spare conscience the dilemmas of its more significant, problematic implications.

Eunoia is celebrated as a form of work. *Eunoia* is attacked as a form of work. Soon after *Eunoia* wins the Griffin Prize in 2002, a parody entitled *Annoya*, under the pseudonym Constrained Balks, appears in the mailboxes of Toronto poets. *Annoya*'s rhetorical goal is specifically to diminish the labour legend of *Eunoia*, by making Bök's book seem easy to write. As reviewer Alex Good ruminates: "It couldn't have taken seven years to come up with stuff like this. Seven minutes with a good dictionary would do the trick" (Rev. of Bök). (The occult number 7 flashes through the reviews like a numerological beacon, a magical fetish.) Similarly, *Eunoia* is attacked as unproductive play, rather than a "serious work" of poetry. Play, even it is accumulative in other ways and libidinally re-warding, can only accrue limited value; play is never cruel enough, never violent enough, to be virtuous. Pseudonymous reviewer Clive Staples – the name is taken from C.S. Lewis, whose full name is Clive Staples Lewis – contrasts more valuable work-like play to valueless, frivolous forms of play: "Traditional poetic forms (including the hardest of them all – free verse) are like chess. Lipograms are like tic-tac-toe" ("Letter"). Chess is rehearsal for war, combative logic and martial ritual; tic-tac-toe is an effete, mushy-headed pastime. Even if Clive Staples is possibly Bök parodying his antagonists, the parody is exact. More invested detrac-tors, like Lynda Grace Philippsen, cannot understand "why someone of [Bök's] obvious ingenuity should choose to spend seven years on such masochistic infliction. (Or is that affliction?)" ("Letter"). To Philippsen, Bök has wasted precious life energy, talent and time. She implies that if a stupid person were to behave this way, it would be understandable. Of course, says ideology. But someone of such "obvious ingenuity"? When a talented poet writes in another mode of value than the reviewer's own, it is a tragic annoyance. Or, as Alex Good writes: "You're always left with the big tease of its conception: Why did Christian Bök choose to write a book like this?" (Rev. of Bök). Starnino asks: "All well and good, but why would anyone wish to write this way other than for the mere curiosity of it?" ("Vowel Movements"). A curiosity, a toy, unproductive expendi-ture. Useless work. Robert Stacey's tart retort to David Solway's similar question is apt here: "Good and Starnino can't see merit in *Eunoia* be-cause they make no effort to answer their own questions" ("Toil" 65). The referential circularity of the ideolect forecloses their inquiry. Under a paradigm of mimesis, reflection and expression, poetry reviewers often cannot see the "point" of postmodern poetry – what it encrypts. They seek a solution to a riddle that the work does not, in fact, pose. Illiterates of form, all they can say is that: "*Eunoia* doesn't have any kind of purpose or point to it except as an experiment. Its prime directive is the only thing it has to say" (Starnino, "Vowel Movements").

In one case at least, the innocence that the labour legend of *Eunoia* purchases is so great that it produces a serious dilemma for a conscientious reviewer. On the one hand, the form of labour that went into its making gives the poem absolute, unimpeachable value (*Eunoia* stores Quality like a precious electric charge, if ever a Canadian book of poetry has). On the other hand, Bök's aesthetic imperative (as read out of the content) is misguided, pointless, unproductive, or mad. Although his review suggests he did not actually read the book, Lyle Neff finds himself pinched between the pro/con/*say-what?* positions above. He writes, in "Eunnoyance: How the Griffin Decision Favours Effort Over Accomplishment," that:

Eunoia is not a digital piece of work, but represents, one hates to say, a triumph of the (eccentric, human) will. It is painful, when reading it, to think of how hard this man worked on this book.... [But] if we grant that Short Haul Engine *and* Eunoia *are both good books which took some heavy artistic lifting to make, doesn't Solie's book gain the aesthetic upper hand because it is a more buoyant read? (44)*

In this excerpt, Neff posits the conventional antagonism between the inauthentic forces of postmodernity (the "digital") and authentic modern (the "human"). When he discovers that Christian Bök is not the name of an algorithm, he reluctantly admits this poet to the order of the "eccentric, human." Somehow this is in fact more of a threat: "one hates to say ... it is painful." The trope Neff then evokes has much more immediate rhetorical force than that of the plastic/digital: the Third Reich. Neff implies that *Eunoia* is a Nazi-esque, übermenschian "triumph of the ... will." To Neff, Bök is human but possibly psychopathic. Note that Neff never once exits the gift shop paradigm of labour as value. *Eunoia* curiously, amply affirms the labour-as-value-as-Quality ideology through the legend of its construction, to such an extent that he is forced to admit it into the realm of true poetry. Neff is forced to "grant that ... both [are] good books which took some heavy artistic lifting to make." He grants this, reluctantly, in spite of the fact that, when tested in almost all the other terms of the dominant evaluative ideolect, the content of *Eunoia* produces very few unambiguous positives. For example, in a review by Gordon Neufeld, using "trick" as "nonproductive play," as Brian Fawcett did, Neufeld says that: "[*Eunoia* is] little more than a party trick [because] ... if you set aside the fact that Bök uses only one vowel in each section, and examine the work for other poetic merits, it has few" ("Little More"). Neff is stuck with the serious dilemma of how to arrive, conscientiously, at the conclusion that Solie's book is better. He accomplishes this by altering his definition of labour. Neff's actual conclusion is that *Short Haul Engine* is better, and more prizeworthy, because it was, in truth, harder to write than *Eunoia*. Although *Eunoia* may have demanded longer hours at the desk, and a greater blitzkrieg of ingenuity, Solie's genuinely Human form of labour is the more costly, and therefore the more authentic.

Through Canadian Poetry Reviewing

In the Fall of 2003 *The Malahat Review* published a special issue devoted entirely to the subject of book reviewing. Edited by Marlene Cookshaw and Lorna Jackson, the contributors are authors from Canada, Britain and the United States who also publish reviews. A crucial impetus to the creation of the issue was dissatisfaction with book reviewing practices. Most of the documents included in the special issue, consequently, are diagnostic, corrective, critical or constructively negative. This dissatisfaction is not local to *Malahat Review* affiliates: A number of other essays about reviewing published in other Canadian magazines (*Geist*, *The Danforth Review*, *sub-Terrain*, *Canadian Notes and Queries* and elsewhere) and works like Darren Wershler-Henry's *10 out of 10, or, Why poetry criticism sucks in 2003* (2003) confirm that Canadian poets are perpetually unsatisfied with how book reviewing is practiced.

With 22 short essays or "critical notes," the *Malahat* issue is set up to be a noisy roundtable, a thorough semi-formal discussion of a topic dear and dreadful to the participants. With several pieces in dialogic or collaborative form, it does stage a convincing performance of a parliamentary form of debate, giving space to (ostensibly) dissenting, contrasting ideas. John Lent's article "Somebody Paying Attention: Reviewing, the Intellectual, and the Region" sets out with declared negative intent, a promise to ask hard questions about reviewing, and to attack some basic assumptions. Querying the status of the intellectual in Canadian literary culture, Lent comes to suspect

that there is ... a vast, quiet, anti-intellectual malaise in our culture that
interferes with the act of reviewing ... some shy, overly colonized, and
slightly Canadian (i.e., easily embarrassed) side of ourselves does not want
to reveal pure intellectual engagement, even though we admire it so much
in writers from other cultures. (88)

Outside of his formulaic Canadian self-deprecation, it might be antici-
pated that when Lent writes "pure intellectual engagement" in review-
ing, he calls for something that functions outside pallid realms of reified,
mercantile value, outside the phantasmic galleries of Grecian urns and
wax museums, outside the living rooms of retired engineers, and away
from the flesh-burning rituals of sheer work-as-value. Throughout the
piece, Lent repeatedly makes the gesture of starting over, as it were, as
if with each iteration he drills deeper into the problem: "I still haven't
nailed this right" (89). What form of pure intellectual engagement does
he, finally, propose as a solution to lift book reviewing in Canada from
its low state? He proposes a return to *craft*, as if that discourse were ever
in eclipse.

there is not enough knowledge or confidence about knowledge *that has*
to do with knowing enough about composition – *the* crafts *of writing in*
different literary modes and genres – to support a wide field of first-rate
reviewers. (89 emphases in original)

Per Lent, "pure intellectual engagement" (Quality here, as usual, is an
eternal site beyond ideology, one that objective, lawful rational processes
can direct the critic to discover) somehow does not threaten the basic
formula that: criticism = judgement and quality = veracity.

Lent's is only one example in the special issue of non-critical self-re-
flection; self-reflection that doesn't find an escape from its own devices.
By the end of the special issue, the book review has been questioned by
so many voices, from so many ostensibly different perspectives, that one

anticipates it will be left bruised and broken, the reviewer less confident of the review as a means to construct and project aesthetic identity.

Dominant reviewing practices emerge without a scratch, however, because through this entire sustained application of intelligence and erudition, vehemence and enthusiasm – the special issue is over 130 pages long – all the basic tropes, concepts and metaphors of the ideolect remain largely unquestioned. They are invoked and reapplied without critique. As Henri Lefebvre remarked, "Bourgeois thought has never been able to behave critically vis-a-vis its own categories … it has not extracted itself from their fetishistic power" (71). The issue ultimately devolves into a debate over manners. Although the book review genre is questioned, it is questioned from within the terms of the dominant review ideolect – a Royal Mounted Common Sense Police internal investigation.

Judith Butler's "Conscience Doth Make Subjects of Us All" brings me back to aesthetic conscience. For Althusser, she writes:

[T]he efficacy of ideology consists in part in the formation of conscience, *where the notion of conscience is understood to place restrictions on what is speakable or, more generally, representable. Conscience … designates a kind of turning back – a reflexivity – which constitutes the conditions for the possibility of the subject's formation…. Conscience is fundamental to the production and regulation of the citizen subject, for it is conscience that turns the individual around to make itself available to the subjectivating reprimand: a turning back and a turning toward. (13)*

Conscience is all these things and still more than this reflexive turn. Conscience is nothing less than the administrative apparatus of ideology. But the answer to the question of one of the articles' titles "What is a Review Supposed to Do?" is that it is partly (in a sense, both local and global) to make the reviewer and the reviewed available to the subjectivating reprimand. Among the goals of a negative review is the stimulation of the poet's aesthetic conscience with aesthetico-moral emotions. Reviews, in

237

practice, are often rituals of public shaming or criminal branding. To the living poet under review, the reviewer performs as the phantasmic voice of conscience, while being also the possessor, subject and victim of that voice. This is how novelist Michelle Berry accounts her experiences as a reviewer in her contribution to *The Malahat Review* 144: "On Being a Writer Who Is Also a Reviewer." One assumption at work here is that, before she started reviewing, Berry wrote her fiction in an unfettered, spontaneous way. In reviewing, however, aesthetic conscience began to trouble her at the writing desk.

But as I wrote more and more reviews I found it enhanced my fiction writing. Getting out of my mind, seeing how others shaped their work, thinking about the process of writing and noticing the slight movements of thought and technique in a writer's work. I was studying writing again…. There are problems with all of this too, of course. Studying writing again suddenly made me self-conscious about my fiction. It made me aware of everything I was doing as I did it. ("Ah, I've got this water image running through my chapter – is it good or bad? What would a reviewer think of this theme?") (86)

Berry, like several of the contributors, becomes aesthetically conscience-stricken through reviewing, and several of the contributors frame their articles as confessions of guilt. Typically, the ideas or sensibility that introduce the passage promise critique: "[T]hinking about the process of writing and noticing the slight movements of thought and technique in a writer's work." Typically, they also fail to probe their own categories. The processes of aesthetic conscience at work here thus risk becoming self-sufficient, circular in the sense that Hegel named. Too often, the contributors in *Malahat* 144 go through an elaborate introspection only to arrive, exhausted, back at the familiar aesthetico-moral referendum: Is it good or is it bad? Round and round.

Jan Zwicky's piece, "The Ethics of the Negative Review," is at least a much fuller extrapolation from the questions posed by the aesthetic conscience than Berry's mere hint, or the revising-on-the-go of Lent's anxiety. Zwicky's is a long internal dialogue of the self "Jan Zwicky" and the aesthetic conscience of "Jan Zwicky." As Zwicky is the author of over 10 poetry collections, a Governor General's Award winner and a professor of philosophy at the University of Victoria, the article looks promising. And if the practice of philosophy is about changing the terms of debate, asking critical questions, one might at least expect a philosophy professor to turn her assumptions back on themselves. So what does Zwicky's aesthetic conscience finally answer? She concludes that "negative" reviewing is impossible because reviewers who damn books "need to be sure beyond a reasonable doubt, each time we take up the rhetorical cudgels, that our judgement is going to stand the test of time. And frankly … I don't think we *can* be that sure" (55). Again and again the futile God-quest for certainty hog ties aesthetic reasoning into the circularity of its own devices.

These three reviewers have competent aesthetic consciences – overly competent. None fulfil their declared promises to tread on fundamental assumptions. Zwicky answers the question about reviewing and value, which she frames with the chestnut: "The critics killed Keats" (54), in value's terms. The assumption of permanent value in Quality (the moral ideal of aesthetic conscience) is never in question. Neither is there ever a question that the project of literature is the production of (writer-side) and ascent (reviewer-side) of Mount Everest-like Greatnesses: "*Great* literature … couldn't require boundary police to insure a readership. That of its own accord it continues to inspire whomever comes in contact with it is precisely in what its 'greatness' consists" (56). The question remains the evaluative reviewer's question, that of a closed, efficacious aesthetic conscience: do "positive" or "negative" reviews contribute more to the cultural process of "culling" (Dessaux 96)? Most of the time a wakeful aesthetic conscience only functions to refine, elaborate and strengthen dominant ideology, even when the moral agent sets out, sincerely, to challenge it. Unless the ideolect itself is challenged or abandoned, contrasted voices can perform as the complementary supports (yin and yang?) of the same ideology. Two of the pieces in *Malahat* 144 read that way: Debates between writers who may as well be the right hand and the left hand of the same church organist. As Lefebvre writes: "The poles are both opposed and mutually supporting. All this diversity represents a process of opposition within a unified whole" (73).

Yet aesthetic conscience does have liberatory potential. It has whatever liberatory potential art itself has. Although it can become circular, conscience, as Koops *et al.* suggest, can also "guide us outside of awareness" (5). The processes of *aesthetic* conscience gain more liberatory potential by constant contact with art's considerable social powers. Michèle Barrett quotes Marxist aesthetic philosopher Max Raphael on this point: "Art frees us from enslavement to words, concepts and false moral values by showing us that life knows differentiations that cannot be reduced to concepts as well as situations which cannot be judged by accepted moral standards" (705).

In what circumstances, and how, does aesthetic conscience break out of its own circuits? When and how does it become a *critical*, not merely a *reflective* (or circular), process? On the level of discourse, the principal question is that of the unconscious, spontaneous character of ideology. Current theorization of embedded metaphor and ideology confirm the basic Gramscian argument that assumptions are more determining when invisible, unconscious. As Andrew Goatly writes: "it is precisely because they are conventionalized that they may achieve the power to subconsciously affect our thinking, without our being aware of it" (*Washing* 22). If so, the very process of aesthetic deliberation provoked by art dilemmas can potentially bring the assumptions, the embedded guiding metaphors, up to the light of conscious scrutiny. At that point, assumptions often become explosive in the discovery that significance in art always exceeds what is predictable by historical awareness, artistic intent and conscientious imperative. Steve McCaffery writes of the aporia of metaphor in "Writing as a General Economy." The micro-mechanisms of metaphor he outlines map onto those of conscientious deliberation:

The semantic mechanism is rendered nomadic; meaning wanders from one term to another and any relationship through substitution and equivalence can only be asserted within the framing and staging of a certain loss. (204)

The potential in aesthetic deliberation is that this loss, as it discharges from the nomadic drift of metaphor, might be discovered, and throw the subject of conscience somewhere beyond ideological guarantee – a discursive landmine inside the critic's own language. Once brought to light in such ways, the reified categories of an ideolect can be stripped of their fetishistic power.

As suggested above, through its unbroken connection with art, with the rabble of the senses, aesthetic conscience already holds more promise of rupture than sheer moral conscience. Affect, as a primary component of conscience, is among the unruly powers that ensures the presence of contradictions, of hypocrisy, and the unpredictability of what developmental psychologists call "moral outcomes" – which I might call poetic "value outcomes." Contra Althusser, not all feelings will answer the interpellative call of reason. New, internally antagonistic identitarian convictions can be developed which force conscience to adjust. Because ideology is never perfectly determinate, competence is never perfectly circular. Hegel's hard heart is in paralysis. Shaftesbury's virtuoso is an hypothetical type. Goethe's beautiful soul is a narcissistic psychopath. So conscience's structure, which is a shifting relationship of already dynamic components, is gappy, porous, riddled with openings that critical intelligence, once activated, can worm its way through.

Furthermore, conscience is empty and hungry, with a territorial avarice that compels it to annex human sensory experience. To Nietzsche, although conscience once acted as Christianity's ideological administration, its structural imperatives led, finally, to its own downfall. Filled with the content of pious Christian morality, conscience by its very hunger chews its way out of its original strictures. In *The Gay Science*, Nietzsche writes:

You see what actually conquered the Christian God; Christian morality itself, the concept of truthfulness which was taken more and more seriously; the confessional punctiliousness of Christian conscience, translated and sublimated into scientific conscience, into intellectual rigour at any price. (162)

Thus the emptiness of conscience holds further promise still: The entire moral basis of conscience can potentially be re-created as an result of its own processes, with new affective, identitarian, or discursive grounds. Aesthetic conscience can mutate to work toward utopian ends, rather than value-conservative ends. Without the coming-to-voice of common sense that occurs within aesthetic conscience, the potential to bring the organising categories under critical scrutiny, the spontaneous assumptions that undergird dominant cultural ideology go unchallenged. Any hope of shifting the dominant reviewer's ideolect in Canada thus lies entirely within the domain of aesthetic conscience, and will only emerge through a transformed practice of book reviewing. In Terry Eagleton's words, in "The Ideology of the Aesthetic:"

The aesthetic is at once eloquent testimony to the enigmatic origins of morality in a society which everywhere violates it and a generous utopian glimpse of an alternative to this sorry condition. For what the aesthetic imitates ... is nothing less than human existence itself which needs no rationale beyond its own self-delight, which is an end in itself and which will stoop to no external determination. (338)

Works Cited

Articles, Books and Other

Achugar, Hugo. "The Book of Poems as Social Act." *Marxism and the Interpretation of Culture*. Eds. Cary Nelson and Lawrence Grossberg. Urbana: U of Illinois P, 1988. 651–62. Print.

Ahmed, Sarah. "The Economy of Affect." *Social Text* 22.2 (2004): 117–139. Print.

Althusser, Louis. "Ideology and Ideological State Apparatuses." *Lenin and Philosophy and Other Essays*. Trans. Ben Brewster. New York and London: Monthly Rev. P, (1971): 127–186. Print.

——. "Part Seven. Marxism and Humanism." *Marxists.org*. [no date]. Web. 8 July 2008.

Altieri, Charles. "From Symbolist Thought to Immanence: The Ground of Postmodern American Poetics." *boundary* 2. 1.1/3. Spring (1973): 605–642. Print.

Antin, David. "Modernism and Postmodernism: Approaching the Present in American Poetry." *boundary* 2. 1/1. Autumn (1972): 98–133. Print.

Bahktin, Mikhail. *The Dialogic Imagination*. Austin: U of Austin P, 1981. Print.

Barrett, Michèle. "The Place of Aesthetics in Marxist Criticism." *Marxism and the Interpretation of Culture*. Eds. Cary Nelson and Lawrence Grossberg. Urbana: U of Illinois P, 1988. 697–714. Print.

Barthes, Roland. *S/Z*. Trans. Richard Miller. New York: Hill and Wang, 1974. Print.

——. *Writing Degree Zero*. Trans. Annette Lavers and Colin Smith. New York: Hill and Wang, 1968. Print.

————. "From Work to Text." Trans. Richard Howard. *The Critical Tradition*. Ed. David H. Richter. New York: Bedford/St. Martins, 1998. 901–905. Print.

Barzun, Jacques. *The Culture We Deserve*. Wesleyan UP, 1989. Print.

Bayne, Peter. *Lessons from My Masters, Carlyle, Tennyson and Ruskin*. New York: Harper & Brothers, 1879. Print.

Bernstein, Charles. "Interview with Charles Bernstein" *The Front Table*. Seminary Co-op Bookstore. February/March 1999. Web. 8 July 2008.

Betts, Gregory. "Postmodern Decadence." *Re: Reading the Postmodern*. Ed. Robert David Stacey. Ottawa: U of Ottawa P, 2010. 151–182. Print.

Billig, Michael and Katie MacMillan. "Metaphors, Idiom and Ideology." *Discourse & Society* 16.4 (2005): 459–480. Print.

Blaser, Robin. "Introduction." *Particular Accidents: Selected Poems by George Bowering*. Vancouver: Talonbooks, 1980. Print.

Blodgett, E. D. *Five-Part Invention: A History of Literary History in Canada*. Toronto: U of Toronto P, 2003. Print.

Bök, Christian. *Eunoia*. Toronto: Coach House Books, 2001. Print.

Bök, Christian and Carmine Starnino. "The Cage Match of Canadian Poetry." Mount Royal University, Calgary, 26 November 2009. Live debate. Available online: http://vimeo.com/7963755. Web. 26 January 2012.

Bourdieu, Pierre. *The Field of Cultural Production*. New York: Columbia UP, 1993. Print.

————. *The Rules of Art: Genesis and Structure of the Literary Field*. Trans. Susan Emanuel. Cambridge: Polity, 1996. Print.

————. "The Work of Art as Fetish: The Production of Belief." *Text & Context: A Journal of Interdisciplinary Studies* 2.1 (1988): 3–56. Print.

Burnham, Clint. "Anxieties, Orthodoxies, and History in (the 1990s Critical Reception of) bpNichol's The Martyrology." *Open Letter* 13.8 (2009): 19–28. Print.

Butler, Judith. "Conscience Doth Make Subjects of Us All." *Yale French Studies* 88 June (1995): 6–26. Print.

Butling, Pauline. "Mess is Lore." *Re: Reading the Postmodern*. Ed. Robert David Stacey. Ottawa: U of Ottawa P, 2010. 313–335. Print.

Callinicos, Alex. *Against Postmodernism: A Marxist Critique*. Cambridge: Polity, 1989. Print.

Davey, Frank. *Surviving the Paraphrase: Eleven Essays On Canadian Literature*. Winnipeg: Turnstone, 1983. Print.

————. "Canadian Canons." *Critical Inquiry*. 16:3 Spring (1990): 672–681. Print.

————. *From There to Here: A Guide to English-Canadian Literature Since 1960*. Erin Village, Ontario: Porcépic, 1974. Print.

————. *Mr. and Mrs. G. G*. Toronto: E C W, 2003. Print.

Derksen, Jeff. "Where Have All the Equal Signs Gone?" *Assembling Alternatives: Reading Postmodern Poetries Transnationally*. Ed. Romana Huk. Middletown, Conn: Wesleyan UP, 2003. 41–46. Print.

Despland, Michel. "Can Conscience Be Hypocritical? The Contrasting Analyses of Kant and Hegel." *The Harvard Theological Review* 68: 3/4 (1975): 357–370. Print.

Eagleton, Terry. "Introduction." *Ideology*. New York: Longman, 1994. Print.

————. *Ideology : An Introduction*. London; New York: Verso, 1991. Print.

————. "The Ideology of the Aesthetic." *Poetics Today* 9:2 (1988): 327–338. Print.

————. "From the Polis to Postmodernism." *The Ideology of the Aesthetic*. London: Blackwell, 1990. 366–417. Print.

Eliot, T.S. "Tradition and the Individual Talent." *The Critical Tradition*. Ed. David Richter. New York: Bedford/St.Martins, 1998: 498–503. Print.

Fish, Stanley. "French Theory in America." *NewYorkTimes.com* 6 April 2008. Web. 6 July 2008.

————. "How Ordinary is Ordinary Language?;" "How to Recognise a Poem When You See One." *Is There a Text in this Class?* New York:

Harvard UP, 1980. 97–111; 322–337. Print.

Foster, Hal. *Design and Crime*. London: Verso, 2002. Print.

Goatly, Andrew. *Washing the Brain: Metaphor and Hidden Ideology*. Amsterdam; Philadelphia: John Benjamins, 2007. Print.

—————. "Ideology and Metaphor." *English Today* 87. 22:3 July (2006): 25–39. Print.

Golding, Sue. "The Concept of the Philosophy of Praxis in the Quaderni of Antonio Gramsci." *Marxism and the Interpretation of Culture*. Eds. Cary Nelson and Lawrence Grossberg. Urbana: U of Illinois P, 1988. 542–563 Print.

Gram, Moltke S. "Moral and Literary Ideals in Hegel's Critique of 'The Moral World-View.'" *The Phenomenology of Spirit Reader*. Ed. Jon Stewart. New York: State U of New York P, 1998. 307–333. Print.

Gramsci, Antonio. *The Antonio Gramsci Reader*. Ed. David Forgacs. New York: New York UP, 2000. Print.

Grossberg, Lawrence. "Rereading the Past From the Future." *International Journal of Cultural Studies* 10:1 (2007): 125–133. Print.

Guillory, John. "The Ideology of Canon Formation: T.S. Eliot and Cleanth Brooks." *Critical Inquiry* 10:1 September (1983): 173–198. Print.

Habermas, Jürgen. "Modernity-An Incomplete Project." *The Anti-Aesthetic*. Ed. Hal Foster. Seattle: Bay, 1983: 3–15. Print.

Hall, Stuart. "The Problem of Ideology: Marxism Without Guarantees." *Stuart Hall: Critical Dialogues in Cultural Studies*. Eds. David Morley and Kuan-Hsing Chen. New York: Routledge, 1996: 25–46. Print.

Hegel, G.W.F. *Phenomenology of Spirit*. Trans. A.V. Miller. New York: Oxford UP, 1977. Print.

Hutcheon, Linda. *A Poetics of Postmodernism*. New York: Routledge, 1988. Print.

Jameson, Fredric. "Postmodernism, or, The Cultural Logic of Late Capitalism." *The Jameson Reader*. Eds. Hardt, Michael and Weeks, Kathi. Malden, Mass: Blackwell, 2000. Print.

—————. "On Interpretation: Literature as a Socially Symbolic Act."

The Jameson Reader. Eds. Michael Hardt and Kathi Weeks. Malden, Mass: Blackwell, 2000. Print.

——. "Towards Dialectical Criticism." *The Jameson Reader*. Eds. Michael Hardt and Kathi Weeks. Malden, Mass: Blackwell, 2000. Print.

——. "The Barrier of Time." *Archaeologies of the Future*. London: Verso, 2005; 2007. 85–106. Print.

Keller, Monika et al. "'Happy' and 'Unhappy' Victimizers: The Development of Moral Emotions from Childhood to Adolescence." *The Development and Structure of Conscience*. Eds. Willem Koops et al. New York: Psychology P, 2010. 253–68. Print.

Koops et al. "The Development of Conscience: Concepts and Theoretical and Empirical Approaches. An Introduction." *The Development and Structure of Conscience*. Eds. Willem Koops et al. New York: Psychology P, 2010. 1–23. Print.

Kraus, Rosalind. "Sculpture in the Expanded Field." *The Anti-Aesthetic*. Ed. Hal Foster. Seattle: Bay, 1983: 31–42. Print.

Laclau, Ernesto. "Metaphor and Social Antagonisms." *Marxism and the Interpretation of Culture*. Eds. Cary Nelson and Lawrence Grossberg. Urbana: U of Illinois P, 1988. 249–58. Print.

Lakoff, George and Mark Johnson. *Metaphors We Live By*. Chicago: University of Chicago Press, 1980. Print.

Lefebvre, Henri. *Key Writings*. Eds. Stuart Elden et al. New York: Continuum, 2003. Print.

Lehman, David. *The Last Avant-Garde: The Making of the New York School of Poets*. New York: Doubleday, 1998. Print.

Léon, María José Alcaraz. "The Rational Justification of Aesthetic Judgments." *Journal of Aesthetics and Art Criticism* 66.3 (2008): 291–300. Print.

Mancini, Donato. Journal Entry. January 23, 2006. [no pagination]. Print.

Mansbridge, Peter. "A Computer Network Called Internet." *CBC.ca*. October 8, 1993. Web. 8 July 2008.

Marx, Karl. *Capital*. Trans. Samuel Moore and Edward Aveling. London:

Encyclopedia Britannica, 1952. Print.

McCaffery, Steve. "Writing as a General Economy." *Artifice & Indeterminacy: An Anthology of New Poetics*. Ed. Christopher Beach. Tuscaloosa: U of Alabama P, 1998. 201–221. Print.

McClatchy, J.D. "Introduction." *The Vintage Book of Contemporary American Poetry*. Ed, J.D. McClatchy. New York: Vintage, 2003. Print.

McFarland, Thomas. *The Masks of Keats*. New York: Oxford UP, 2000. Print.

Middleton, Peter. "Imagined Readerships & Innovation in U.K. Poetry." *Assembling Alternatives: Reading Postmodern Poetries Transnationally*. Ed. Romana Huk. Middletown, Conn: Wesleyan UP, 2003. 127–141. Print.

Miki, Roy. *Broken Entries: Race, Subjectivity, Writing: Essays*. Toronto: Mercury P, 1998. Print.

Moore, T. Sturge. *Albert Durer*. Whitefish, MT: Kessinger P, 2004. Print.

Musschenga, Bert. "Moral Violations and the Ordinary Moral Person." *The Development and Structure of Conscience*. Eds. Willem Koops et al. New York: Psychology Press, 2010. 25–48. Print.

Myles, John. "From Habitus to Mouth: Language and Class in Bourdieu's Sociology of Language." *Theory and Society* 28.6 December (1999): 879–901. Print.

Nietzsche, Friedrich. *On the Genealogy of Morality*. Trans. Carol Diethe. Cambridge: Cambridge UP, 2007. Print. [edition includes sections from *Daybreak*; *The Gay Science*; *Beyond Good and Evil*]

————. *Human, All Too Human*. Trans. R. J. Hollingdale. Cambridge: Cambridge UP, 1996. Print.

O'Brien, Susie and Imre Szeman. "The Globalization of Fiction/the Fiction of Globalization." *The South Atlantic Quarterly* 100.3 (2001): 603–626. Print.

Olsen, Stein Haugom. "Value Judgments in Criticism." *Journal of Aesthetics and Art Criticism* 42.2 (1983): 125–136. Print.

Olthof, Tjeert. "Conscience in the Classroom: Early Adolescents' Moral Emotions, Moral Judgements, and Moral Identity as Predictors of their Interpersonal Behavior." *The Development and Structure of Conscience*. Eds. Willem Koops et al. New York: Psychology P, 2010. 327–342. Print.

Patterson, Robert Hogarth. "Real and Ideal Beauty." *Essays In History and Art*. London: W. Blackwood and Sons, 1862. 44–101. Print.

Paz, Octavio. *On Poets and Others*. New York: Arcade, 1990. Print.

Perelman, Bob. "The New Sentence in Theory and Practice." *American Literature* 65.2 June (1993): 313–324. Print.

————. "Poetry in Theory." *Diacritics* 26 3/4 (1996): 158–175. Print.

————. "Polemic Greeting to the Inhabitants of Utopia." *Assembling Alternatives: Reading Postmodern Poetries Transnationally*. Ed. Romana Huk. Middletown, Conn.: Wesleyan UP, 2003. 375–383. Print.

————. "Write the Power." *American Literary History* 6.2 (1994): 306–324. Print.

Reed, Christopher. "Making History: The Bloomsbury Group's Construction of Aesthetic and Sexual Identity." *Gay and Lesbian Studies in Art History*. Ed. Whitney Davis. New York: Routledge, 1994. 189–224. Print.

Roumanes, Jacques-Bernard. "La conscience esthétique." *Vie des Arts* 44 (1999–2000): 28–9. Print.

Shklovsky, Victor. "Art as Device." *Theory of Prose*. Trans. Benjamin Sher. Normal, IL: Dalkey Archive P, 1991. 1–15. Print.

Smith, Barbara Hernstein. "Contingencies of Value." *The Critical Tradition*. Ed. David H. Richter. New York: Bedford/St.Martins, 1998. 1551–1575. Print.

Spahr, Juliana. "Introduction." *Everybody's Autonomy: Connective Reading and Collective Identity*. Tuscaloosa: U of Alabama P, 2001. Print.

Stacey, Robert David. "Introduction: Post-, Marked Canada." *Re: Reading the Postmodern*. Ed. Robert David Stacey. Ottawa: U of Ottawa P, 2010. xi–xxxv. Print.

————. "Toil and Trouble: On Work in Christian Bök's *Eunoia*." *Canadian Poetry: Studies, Documents, Reviews* 62 (2008): 64–79. Print.

Terwogt et al. "Children's feelings and evaluations about altruistic and self-serving lies." *The Development and Structure of Conscience.* Eds. Willem Koops et al. New York: Psychology P, 2010. 207–220. Print.

van de Velde, Henry. "Memoirs: 1891–1901." *Theories of Modern Art: A Source Book by Artists and Critics.* Eds. Herschel Browning Chipp et al. Los Angeles: U of California P, 1968. 120–123. Print.

Warner, Michael. "Publics and Counterpublics." *Public Culture* 14:1 (2002): 49–90. Print.

Williams, Raymond. "The Creative Mind." *The Long Revolution.* New York: Harper Torchbooks, 1966. 3–40. Print.

Yevtushenko, Yevgeny. "I Journeyed Through Russia." *The Penguin Book of Socialist Verse.* Ed. Alan Bold. London: Penguin, 1970. 480–488. Print.

Žižek, Slavoj. *The Plague of Fantasies.* London: New York: Verso, 1997. Print.

————. *Welcome to the Desert of the Real!* New York: Verso, 2002. Print.

Reviews and Review-Essays

Acorn, Milton. "Avoid the Bad Mountain." *Blackfish* 3 (1972): [no pagination]. Print.

Almon, Burt. "The Sincerity Test." *Canadian Literature* 184 (2005): 145. Print.

Archer, Bert and Gartner, Zuszsi. "True Confessions: An Email Debate on Perfectly Agreeable Books and Other Perils of the Trade." *The Malahat Review* 144 (2003): 23–34. Print.

Aubert, Rosemary. "109 Poets." *The Tamarack Review* 8/82 (1981): 94–99. Print.

Badman, Derik. "*Eunoia* by Christian Bok." Rev. of *Eunoia* by Christian Bök. Weblog entry. *Madinkbeard*. October 11, 2004. Web. 8 July 2008.

Baglow, John. Rev. of *Said Like Reeds or Things* by Marc Truscott. *The Danforth Review*. [no date.] Web. 8 December 2005.

Barbour, Douglas. "Three Horsemen Ride Far and Wide Over the Fields of Discourse." *Event* 10.2 (1987): 101–107. Print.

Basilieres, Michel. Rev. of *Eunoia* by Christian Bök. *The Danforth Review*. [no date].Web. 8 July 2008.

Berry, Michelle. "On Being A Writer Who is Also a Reviewer." *The Malahat Review* 144 (2003): 85–87. Print.

Bolster, Stephanie. "Surviving Survival" *The Northern Poetry Review*. [no date] Web. 6 March 2008.

Carpenter, David. "Stone Chipped and HammerEd." *CV II*. 2.2 (1976): 119–120. Print.

Chan, Weyman. Rev. of *Year Zero* by Brian Henderson. *Dandelion* 23.1 (1996): 83–86. Print.

Colombo, John R. Rev. of *Tish* and *Cataract*. *Canadian Forum*. Dec. (1961): 202–03. Print.

Crawley, Dennis. Rev. of *Eunoia* by Christian Bök. *Quill & Quire* 67 (2001): 40. Print.

Currie, Sheldon. "Intense Pleasure." Rev. of *Intense Pleasure* by David McFadden. *The Antigonish Review* 11 (1972): 110–111. Print.

Dessaux, Robert. "Homo Economicus." *The Malahat Review* 144 (2003): 92–97. Print.

"Eunoia." *Publisher's Weekly*. No. 248.47. Nov 19, 2001: 64(1). Print.

Fawcett, Brian. "East Van Uber Alles?" *Unusual Circumstances, Interesting Times*.Vancouver: New Star, 1991. Print.

—————. "The Conditions of Poetry in Canada." NMFG 25 (1978): [no pagination]. Print.

Francis, Wynne. Rev. of books by Waddington, Beissel, Scott, Layton, and Cohen. *The Tamarack Review*. Spring (1967): 78–86. Print.

Gatenby, Greg. "Poetry Chronicle." *The Tamarack Review*. Summer (1979): 77–94. Print.

Goldsmith, Kenneth. "Information Management." *Poetry Foundation. org.* 01.22.07–01.26.07. Web. 8 July 2008.

Gom, Leona. Rev. of *Domestic Fuel* by Erin Mouré. *Event* 14.2 (1985): 146–147. Print.

Good, Alex. "*Eunoia* by Christian Bök." Rev. of *Eunoia* by Christian Bök. *Good Reports*. [no date]. 6 July 2008. Web.

Grubisic, Katia. Rev. of *Viral Suite* by Mari-Lou Rowley. *Vallum*. (2004). Web. 8 July 2008.

Harry, Margaret. "Standing Apart." *The Antigonish Review* 55 (1983): 71–74. Print.

Holmes, Michael. "Beautiful Thinking." *Toronto Star*. Sunday, February 3, 2002 (Ontarion Edition): D14. Print.

Irie, Kevin. Rev. of *Low Water Slack* by Tim Bowling. *The Antigonish Review* 107 (1996): 151–152. Print.

Johnson, Ingrid. "*Eunoia*: Poetry and Wordplay." Rev. of *Eunoia* by

Christian Bök. *Young Adult Review* 8.1 (2002): 57. Print.

Jurdjevic, Deborah. "Review of *Memories Have Tongue* by Afua Cooper." *Canadian Woman Studies* 13.3 (1993): 108–109. Print.

Lahey, Anita. Rev. of *Running in Prospect Cemetery: New and Selected Poems* by Susan Glickman. *The Malahat Review* 149 (2004): 81–83. Print.

Laird, Steven. Rev. of poetry books nominated for the Governor General's Award in 2007. *Canadian Notes and Queries* 71 (2007): 21–22. Print.

Lane, Patrick. "The Saskatchewan Presses." *Grain* 4.9 (1981): 52–56. Print.

Lent, John. "Somebody Paying Attention: Reviewing, the Intellectual, and the Region." *The Malahat Review* 144 (2003): 88–91. Print.

Lesk, Andrew. "Beautiful Feeling?" *ARC* 49 (2002): 79–80. Print.

Levenson, Christopher. "Five Anthologies." *Canadian Literature* 176 (2003): 134–137. Print.

Lillard, Charles. Rev. of books by Marlatt and Minden and McNeil. *The Malahat Review* 38 (1976): 144–150. Print.

Lyon, Annabel. "What's A Review Supposed to Do?" *The Malahat Review* 144 (2003): 35. Print.

Mathews, Robin. Rev. of books by Davey and Miller. *The Canadian Forum*. September (1962): 143. Print.

MacSween, R.J. Rev. of *Turned Clay* by Cheng Sait Chia. *The Antigonish Review* 48 (1982): 101–102. Print.

McCaffery, Steve. "Rebutal [sic] Critical Responsibilities." *Books in Canada*. Dec. (1990). Web. 8 July 2008.

McCartney, Sharon. Rev. of *The Whole Elephant* by Marlene Cookshaw. *The Malahat Review* 91 (1990): 105–106. Print.

McLaren, Leah. "Vowel Language." *Globe and Mail*. October 30, 2001: NA. Print.

mclennan, rob. [sic] Rev. of *The Centre* by Barry McKinnon. *The Antigonish Review* 141. Web. 8 July 2008.

Moore, Nathaniel G. Rev. of books by Scott and Tamaki. *The Danforth Review*. [no date]. Web. 8 July 2008.

Mullins, Andrew and McDonagh, Patrick. "A Poet's Life." *McGill News Alumni Quarterly*. Winter (1997). Web. 8 July 2008.

Musgrave, Susan. Rev. of books by Ondaatje, Purdy, Kogawa and Bowering. *The Malahat Review* 31 (1974). Print.

Neff, Lyle. "Eunnoyance: How the 2002 Griffin Decision Favours Effort Over Accomplishment." *Sub-Terrain* 35 (2002): 44. Print.

——. "Introducing Five New Vancouver Writers." *Books in Canada*. 2006. Accessed July 08, 2008. Web.

Neilson, Shane. "*Poetry for Dummies: A Reference for the Rest of Us* by John Timpane and Maureen Watts." *The Danforth Review*. [no date.] Accessed December 8, 2005. Web.

——. Rev. of *Surrender* by Roy Miki. *The Danforth Review*. [no date.] Web. 8 December 2005.

Neufeld, Gordon. "Little more than a party trick." *Amazon.com*. 2005. Web. 8 July 2008.

Newton, Stuart. Rev. of books by Daphne Marlatt and John Robert Colombo. *West Coast Review* 10.2 (1975): 66–68. Print.

——. Rev. of books by Mona Fertig, Henry Rappaport, and Edwin Varney. *Event* 7.1 (1978): 139–142. Print.

Osborne, Patty. Rev. of *Eunoia* by Christian Bök. *Geist* 44 (2002). Web. 8 July 2008.

Philippsen, Lynda Grace. "Letter to the Editor." *Books in Canada*. [no date]. Web. 8 July 2008.

Precosky, Don. "Like a Dog in a Cartoon." *Event* 19.13 (1990): 112–115. Print.

Purdy, Al. "Aiming Low." *The Tamarack Review*. Spring (1968): 81–96. Print.

——. Rev. of books by Gilbert, Kiyooka, and Gilbert. *The Canadian Forum*. Sept. (1964): 141–143. Print.

Querengesser, Neil. Rev. of books by Dupré, Powe, and Shenfeld. *Canadian Literature* 193 (2007): 129–131. Print.

Redhill, Michael. "At Play in the Fields of the Word." *Globe & Mail*. Saturday, November 10, 2001: D10. Print.

Rotstein, Jason Ranon Uri. Rev. of *Anatomy of Keys* by Steven Price. *PoetryReviews.ca*. Web. 8 July 2008.

Ruebsaat, Norbert. "Dear Robert (An Open Letter)." Rev. of *Completed Field Notes* by Robert Kroetsch. *Event* 19.1 (1990): 119–123. Print.

Sandler, Linda. "Gustafson & Others." *The Tamarack Review* 62 (1974): 89–94. Print.

Serafin, Bruce. "Colonial Mentalities." *Books in Canada*. Nov. (1990). Web. 8 July 2008.

Shaidle, Kathy. Rev. of *Grand Gnostic Central* by Bryan Sentes. *The Danforth Review*. [no date.] Web. 8 July 2008.

Shea, Theresa. "Review of *Blue Marrow* by Louise Bernice Halfe." *Quill & Quire* 64.6 (1998): 55. Print.

Shreve, Sandy. "How Poems Work: Barbara Nickel." *Globe and Mail*. Web. 8 July 2008.

Smith, Mark J. "Poetic Poppycock." Letter. *Globe and Mail*. Saturday, March 1, 2003: A-18. Print.

Smith, Stephen. "The Chirp Bird on the Rhinoceros." *The Malahat Review* 144 (2003): 103–106. Print.

Snyder, J.K. Rev. of books by Cogswell, Donlan, and Lane. *The Antigonish Review* 84 (1991): 155–165. Print.

Solway, David. "The Great Disconnect." *Director's Cut*. Porcupine's Quill. Erin ON, 2003. 137–209. Print.

Staples, Clive. "Letter to the Editor." *Books in Canada*. [No date]. Web. 8 July 2008.

Starnino, Carmine. "Vowel Movements: Pointless Toil and Empty Productivity." *Books In Canada* 31.4 (2002). Web. 8 July 2008.

sullivan, d.h. Rev. of books by Howard White, Jim McLean and Lionel Kearns. *Event* 12.2 (1983): 131–134. Print.

Taylor, Rob. "Newlove's 'Long Continual' Legacy." *The Peak*. Accessed July 08, 2008.Web.

Tremblay, Tony. "'Still Burning' … Brightly." *The Antigonish Review* 116. Winter (1999): 11–15. Print.

Various Authors. Letters to the editor regarding *Eunoia*. *Books in Canada*. [no date] Web. 8 July 2008.

Wagner, Linda W. "Four Young Poets." *Ontario Review* 1 (1974): 89–97. Print.

Webb, Phyllis. Rev. of *Poetry 64*. Eds. Jacques Godbout and John Robert Colombo. *The Canadian Forum*. May (1964): 150. Print.

Welch, Liliane. Rev. of books by Hédi Bouraoui and Harry Thurston. *The Antigonish Review* 46 (1981): 108–112. Print.

Wells, Zachariah. "Makin' It Work." *Maissoneuve.org*. June 14, 2004. Web. 8 July 2008.

————. "The Griffin Prize for Stuff Vaguely Resembling Poetry." *Maisonneuve.org*. 17 May 2004. Web. 8 July 2008.

Wood, James. "A Desire to Live By Words: An Email Interview with Lorna Jackson." *The Malahat Review* 144 (2003): 107–113. Print.

Woodcock, George. "Acorn's Remnants." *Event* 19.1 (1990): 100–102. Print.

Zwicky, Jan. "The Ethics of the Negative Review." *The Malahat Review* 144 (2003): 54–63. Print.

Acknowledgements

First of all, I dedicate this book to everyone who works hard for the good and glory of poetry.

The project has been materially made possible by: the Social Sciences and Humanities Research Council; the Simon Fraser University Department of English; the University of British Columbia Department of English; and unusually cheap rent.

My main guides and mentors, at different stages, were Jeff Derksen and Glenn Deer, along with Tom Grieve, Andrew Klobucar, Clint Burnham and Stephen Collis.

Special thanks to Guinevere Pencarrick, there through art-machos, tinfoil rocks, evictionary poodles, sea slug fungus, and a two-year assault from an aswong vampire money cult. General thanks to (variously) lovers, friends, family and critics: Andrea Actis, Rachel Bauman, Pauline Butling, Patrick Foong Chan, Scott Cohen, Wayde Compton, Amy De'Ath, Dunlevy August 2011, Mariam Faqeri, Colin Fulton, Janet Giltrow, John Groot (in memoriam), Margery Fee, Marie Groot, Leah Hokanson, Linda Hutcheon, Andreas Kahre, Amy Kazymerchyk, Larissa Lai, Sasha Langford, Dorothy Trujillo Lusk, François Mancini, Rolf Maurer, Alexander Muir, Heidi Nagtegaal, Nicholas Perrin, Jordan Scott, Colin Smith, Neil Safier, Black Surly, Tim Terhaar, Marie-Hélène Tessier, Aaron Vidaver, James Whitman, Derek Woods, the Kootenay School of Writing Collective(s) and Video In. Big thanks also to the brave Book-Thugs: Jay MillAr and Kate Eichorn, Mark Goldstein, Hazel Millar, Ruth Zuchter, John Schmidt.

And to anyone I have overlooked: thank you.

About the Author

The interdisciplinary practice of Donato Mancini focuses mainly on poetry, bookworks, text-based visual art and cultural criticism. His other books include *Ligatures* (2005), *Æthel* (2007), *Buffet World* (2011) and *Fact 'n' Value* (2011). He is currently a curator in residence in VIVO's Crista Dahl Media Library & Archive, as part of the archival project *Anamnesia: Unforgetting*, and is enrolled in the PhD program in English at the University of British Columbia.

Colophon

Manufactured as the First Edition of *You Must Work Harder to Write Poetry of Excellence* in the Fall of 2012 by BookThug.
Distributed in Canada by the Literary Press Group: www.lpg.ca
Distributed in the U S A by Small Press Distribution: www.spdbooks.org
Shop on-line at www.bookthug.ca

BOOK
PRODUCTION
WAR ECONOMY
STANDARD